SKIRA ART PAPERBACKS

Translated from the French by S.J.C. Harrison

Centennial of VG's birth {

Distributed in the United States by
THE WORLD PUBLISHING COMPANY
2231 West 110th Street, Cleveland, Ohio 44102

Printed in Switzerland in July 1969
by Racine & Glück, La Chaux-de-Fonds, Switzerland

VAN GOGH

Text by

C. H. SIBERT and **CHARLES ESTIENNE**

The Taste of our Time

PAPERBACKS

p 4

CONTENTS

CHRONOLOGICAL SURVEY

1853 **Birth of Vincent Willem Van Gogh, March 30, at the parsonage of Groot Zundert, a village in Dutch Brabant, near the Belgian frontier. Eldest son of Pastor Theodorus, who came of an ancient, much respected Calvinist family, amongst whom we find clergymen; sailors, business men and art-lovers. Three of Vincent's uncles were picture-dealers.**

1856 Eugène Boudin meets young Claude Monet at Le Havre and guides his early efforts.

1857 **May 1: Birth of Theo, Vincent's favorite brother, who is to be his moral and material stand-by to the end of his days.**

1859 Monet and Pissarro meet in Paris. Birth of Seurat.

1860 Large-scale private exhibition in Paris of Modern Painting (Delacroix, Corot, Courbet, Millet).

1861 Edouard Manet shows for the first time at the Salon, and meets Baudelaire. Paul Cézanne's first stay in Paris.

1862 Monet, Renoir and Sisley meet in Paris at Gleyre's studio. Degas paints his first horse races at Longchamp.

1863 Salon des Refusés. Sharp attacks on Manet. Death of Delacroix.

1864 Pissarro exhibits at the Salon, figuring as "Corot's pupil." Birth of Toulouse-Lautrec at Albi.

1865 **Studies at the Provily boarding-school in the neighboring town of Zevenbergen until 1869.**

1865 Manet exhibits "Olympia."

1866 Renoir and Sisley paint together at Marlotte (Forest of Fontainebleau).

1867 Paris World's Fair. Extreme severity of the Salon jury: all the Impressionists are rejected, except Degas. Death of Baudelaire and Ingres. Birth of Pierre Bonnard.

1869 **July 30: Employed at the Goupil art-gallery at The Hague, then at Brussels. Reads much and visits museums.**

1869 Renoir and Monet work at Bougival. The Impressionist technique takes form. Birth of Henri Matisse.

1870 Franco-Prussian War. Proclamation of the Third Republic.

1871 The Paris Commune. Birth of Georges Rouault.

1872 Begins exchanging letters with Theo.

1872 Degas' trip to New Orleans.

1873 May: Transferred to Goupil's London branch, while Theo enters the Brussels office. June: Van Gogh proposes to the daughter of his landlady, Ursula Loyer, with whom he is wildly in love, but she rejects him. Bitter disappointment.

1873 Degas returns to France.

1874 Goes to Paris in October, returns to London in December.

1874 First Group Exhibition of the Impressionists (April 15-May 15); Cézanne is admitted only after difficulties, while Manet abstains.

1875 May: Van Gogh is transferred to headquarters in Paris. Quarrels with the Goupil staff and with customers. His obsession with the Bible begins.

1875 First impressionist sale at the Hôtel Drouot. Death of Corot.

1876 April: Loses his job in Paris. Returns to England as a schoolmaster at Ramsgate, then at Isleworth. Comes home to Etten for Christmas.

1876 Second Group Exhibition of the Impressionists (April). Gauguin is accepted at the official Salon; meets Pissarro and collects impressionist pictures.

1877 January 21-April 30: Clerk in a bookshop at Dordrecht. But Van Gogh is more and more obsessed by his religious vocation and, on May 9, goes to Amsterdam to study for admission to the theological college.

1877 Third Group Exhibition of the Impressionists (April). Cézanne paints at Pontoise with Pissarro, then at Auvers.

1878 July 22: Failing to pass the examination, Van Gogh gives up his studies and returns home. In August he begins a three-months' course at an evangelical training-school at Brussels. On November 15 he is sent out as a lay preacher to the miners in the Borinage. Lodges with a pedlar at Les Pâturages, a townlet near Mons. Shows immense zeal, nurses the sick, sleeps on bare boards.

1878 Paris World's Fair. Duret publishes "Les Peintres impressionnistes."

1879 January: Temporary pastor at Wasmes, in the heart of the black country, but relieved of his duties in July. Period of complete destitution, complete despair.
August: Pastor Pietersen, an amateur watercolorist, buys two drawings from Van Gogh, who is now gradually getting free of his religious obsession.

1879 Fourth Group Exhibition of the Impressionists. Odilon Redon publishes "Dans le rêve," a set of lithographs.

1880 January: Tramps the roads aimlessly. Stops at Courrières, intending to visit the painter Jules Breton, but dares not knock at his door.
Summer: During these anxious months, the darkest of his life, Van Gogh glimpses his artistic vocation. Writes the long, emotional letter to his brother Theo in which he announces his decision to become a painter. Lives at Cuesmes, near Mons in the Borinage. Drawings of miners, copies after Millet.
Brussels (October 1880-April 1881): Lodges at a small hotel, 72, Bd. du Midi. Meets and makes friends with the painter Ridder van Rappard (1858-1892), with whom he corresponds for five years. Lessons in anatomy and perspective. First financial aid from Theo, who is now working for Goupil in Paris.

1880 Fifth Group Exhibition of the Impressionists (April); 18 participants, among them Gauguin.

1881 Etten (April-December): Lives with his parents. Conflicts with his father over his artistic career. Another ill-fated love-affair, with his cousin "K".
The Hague (December 1881-September 1883). Cordially welcomed by his cousin, the painter Mauve, who gives him helpful advice.

1881 Birth of Picasso.

1882 January: Van Gogh picks up in the street a drunken—and pregnant—prostitute, Christine (whom he calls Sien), who serves him as model and companion for twenty months.
March: Van Gogh quarrels with Mauve, who had nevertheless helped him considerably.
June: A stay in hospital. Meets the painter Breitner. Given his first and only order, for 12 pen-and-ink sketches, views of the city. Takes walks to Scheveningen, Woorburg, Leidschendau. Watercolors, lithographs, studies of peasants and fishermen, seascapes, landscapes.

1882 July: He suffers from a feeling that others see in him a nonentity, a disagreeable crank; yet, he protests, "there is in me harmony, calm and music." First oil paintings: the tones are somber, the impasto very thick.

1883 Drenthe (September-November): Stays at Hoogeveen, in a land of moors and peat-bogs. Studies of heath-land, thatched cottages, hamlets, peasants at work.
December: Van Gogh returns to his parents at Nuenen, where his father has been appointed pastor. Sets up his studio in the vicarage barn. Works hard, reads Dickens, Carlyle, Beecher-Stowe.

1883 Death of Manet.

1884 August: Brief idyll with a local girl, Margot, who tries to commit suicide.

1884 Founding of the Salon des Indépendants by Seurat, Signac, Cross and Redon. Gauguin stays at Rouen, then moves to Copenhagen.

1885 March 27: Sudden death of Van Gogh's father. He paints still lifes, peasants, weavers, studies of heads, "The Potato-Eaters" (April-May), "Head of an Old Peasant Woman" (June). "You won't find any silvery tones in my present work, but only brown—bitumen, sepia and the like," he writes in a letter to Theo.
November 23: Leaves for Antwerp. Takes a studio at 194, Rue des Images. Explores the city and harbor, and browses long in antique shops and book-stalls.

1885 Pissarro meets Theo van Gogh, then Signac and Seurat; adopts Pointillism in 1886. Gauguin returns to France in June, meets Degas at Dieppe in August.

1886 January: Discovers Rubens and Japanese prints. Enters the Academy and works under Sieber and Verlat, whose conformist outlook gets on his nerves.
End of February: Van Gogh suddenly decides to go to Paris.
March: Theo welcomes him enthusiastically and puts him up, first in the Rue Laval (now Rue Victor-Massé), then at 54, Rue Lepic. His eyes are opened to bright colors.

1886 June: Enters Cormon's studio where he meets Toulouse-Lautrec. Haunts the Louvre.

> 1886 Eighth and last Group Exhibition of the Impressionists in Paris. Durand-Ruel organizes a large-scale Impressionist Exhibition in New York. Félix Fénéon publishes "Les Impressionnistes en 1886." Gauguin's first stay at Pont-Aven in Brittany, at the Pension Gloanec. Revelation of the Douanier Rousseau at the Indépendants. Rimbaud publishes his "Illuminations."

1887 Influenced by the Impressionists. Often visits Père Tanguy's shop and the Cabaret du Tambourin. Meets Pissarro, Degas, Seurat, Signac and Gauguin. Adopts the pointillist technique for a time.
April: Van Gogh makes friends with Emile Bernard.
June: Enthusiasm for the Japanese prints at the Bing Gallery. His palette grows brighter and his style is changing completely. More than 200 pictures date from this Paris period: self-portraits, still lifes, views of Montmartre and the suburbs, interiors. "The Restaurant" (summer 1887).

> 1887 Gauguin goes to Panama and Martinique with Charles Laval. Toulouse-Lautrec paints his first pictures of Montmartre life. Birth of Juan Gris and Marc Chagall. Mallarmé publishes his "Poésies complètes."

1888 February 20: Leaves suddenly for Arles, on Lautrec's advice. "It's in the South that the studio of the future must be set up." Arles (February 1888-May 1889).
February: Van Gogh puts up at the Restaurant Carrel.
March: Plans an artists' colony. Long exchange of letters with Theo. Death of Mauve.
April: Spring landscapes: "Orchard in Bloom."
May: Moves to a small house, 2 Rue Lamartine, "a yellow house with a tiny white studio."
June: Stays for a week at Saintes-Maries-de-la-Mer. Enraptured by his first sight of the Mediterranean. Paints "Boats on the Beach."
July: Drawings of La Crau, near Montmajour. Pays a visit to his friend the Belgian poet Boch at Fontvieille. — p. 103
August: Becomes friendly with the local postman Roulin and his family, whose portraits he makes. Paints "Sunflowers."
September: Nightscapes and "Outdoor Café at Night."

1888 Between October 20-25: Arrival of Gauguin, who has a great influence on him. Two months of life in common, during which the tension mounts between these two men of fiercely opposed natures.
December: Van Gogh and Gauguin visit Montpellier together to see the works left to the museum by Bruyas.
December 24: Van Gogh attempts to kill Gauguin, then cuts off his own ear. Gauguin hurries back to Paris. Theo arrives. Two weeks' confinement in hospital.

1888 Gauguin's first one-man show at Boussod and Valadon's; his second stay at Pont-Aven; second and, this time, fruitful meeting with Émile Bernard. Beginnings of Cloisonnism and Synthesism. Bonnard, Vuillard, Maurice Denis, Ranson, Paul Sérusier meet at the Académie Julian. Cézanne makes a long stay in Paris. The Belgian painter James Ensor paints his large-scale work: "The Entrance of Christ into Brussels."

1889 January 7: Van Gogh returns to his house. "Self Portrait with Cut Ear," "Still Life with Onions," "La Berceuse."
February: Hallucinations. Hostility of the neighbors. The police are called in, and he is confined again until the end of March. Signac visits him.
April 17: Theo's marriage.
Van Gogh painted 200 pictures during this period, the most fruitful and important of his career.
May 9: At his own request Van Gogh is admitted to the asylum at Saint-Rémy, a townlet near Arles. Dr Rey looks after him. Has two rooms at his disposal and comparative freedom. Long intervals of lucidity between spells of madness.

1889 Paris World's Fair. Construction of the Eiffel Tower. Verlaine publishes "Parallèlement." Gauguin's third stay at Pont-Aven, then at Le Pouldu, where he paints "The Yellow Christ."

1890 January: Birth of Theo's son, Vincent Willem. First article dealing with Van Gogh's work: Albert Aurier's enthusiastic appreciation in Le Mercure de France.
March: One of his pictures, "The Red Vineyard," is sold for 400 francs at the Brussels exhibition of "Les Vingt"; this was the only picture sold during his lifetime.
May 16: Leaves for Paris to visit Theo.

1890 Van Gogh painted 150 pictures during this period of feverishly intense activity: among them "The Cypresses," "The Hospital at Arles," self-portraits and portraits of the asylum staff, "On the Edge of the Alpines," as well as some thirty copies from Millet, Delacroix, Daumier, Rembrandt, Doré.

May 21: Van Gogh arrives at Auvers. Becomes the patient and friend of Dr Gachet, whose portrait he paints. Puts up with Père Ravoux, Place de la Mairie.

July 1: Spends several days in Paris, meets Lautrec again and Albert Aurier. Returns to Auvers and paints "three huge canvases, three far-flung wheatfields under lowering skies"; also, on July 14, "La Mairie d'Auvers."

July 27: In the evening, when in the open country, shoots himself.

July 29: Death of Van Gogh, aged 37, with faithful Theo at his side. His last words were: "There'll never be an end to human misery."

Six months later, on January 25, 1891, Theo died. The brothers lie side by side in the little cemetery at Auvers.

1890 Munch's first stay in Paris, sees pictures by Pissarro, Seurat, Lautrec and, at Theo van Gogh's, works by Gauguin and Vincent van Gogh.

Alfred Vallette launches Le Mercure de France. Bonnard, Vuillard, Denis and Lugné-Poe share a studio at 28 Place Pigalle, Montmartre. Gauguin makes a long stay at Le Pouldu with Séguin, Filiger and Meyer de Haan, returning to Paris in December.

1891 Van Gogh Retrospective Exhibition at the Salon des Indépendants. Death of Seurat. Auction-sale of Gauguin's pictures at the Hôtel Drouot. Gauguin leaves for Tahiti.

This summary has been drawn from the documentary material compiled by Mr Jean Leymarie for The History of Modern Painting (*Skira*, 1949-1950).

CHAPTER ONE

VAN GOGH'S LIFE

— C.H. Sibert

YOUTH

OF broad rather than slender build, with a slight stoop caused by his habit of letting his head hang, his hair cropped short under a straw hat that shaded a strange face... Beneath the faintly-lined forehead and brows knitted in fierce meditation, small, deep-set eyes that at times appeared to be blue, and at others almost green—thus his sister described Vincent Van Gogh in his 'teens. His father, Pastor Theodorus Van Gogh, resident since the year 1849 in the small village of Groot Zundert (Dutch Brabant), had married Anna Cornelia Carbentus, daughter of a book-binder at the Court, in 1851. Vincent, born on March 30, 1853, was the eldest of their six children. Of the others, the best-known, Theo, born in May 1857, was to become the painter's closest friend and ally.

The origins of the Van Gogh family, as far as they can be traced, go back to the 16th century. Its members included goldsmiths, Protestant ministers and even art-dealers. It was a clannish family and, in Vincent's youth, his uncles were to use their influence in helping him to find a settled job.

Vincent was not like other children. He was inclined to be solitary and unsociable. When he went for a walk, he would not allow any of his brothers or sisters, except occasionally Theo, to accompany him. His obstinate and fiery nature was a source of anxiety to his parents.

Van Gogh was educated first at the local school in Groot Zundert and then, from 1865 to 1869, at a boarding-school in Zevenbergen, not far from his native village. But his family was poor and he had to start earning his own living. As he seemed to have no definite ideas on the subject of jobs, one of his uncles, familiarly known as Uncle Cent, who was in charge of an art-gallery at The Hague, found him employment in the same town at a branch of the Goupil art-gallery, a business with headquarters in Paris. He started as a clerk in July 1869, and his duties consisted in unpacking books and dealing with reproductions. He explored the various museums in the town, and his taste for literature and painting developed.

In August 1872 he spent his holidays with his parents, who had moved to Oosterwijck, and came into contact again with his brother Theo, then fifteen years of age. In the close correspondence which sprang up between them following his departure, Vincent sought to interest his younger brother in his own tastes and ideas. From this period onwards, his letters took the characteristic form of long monologues, appeals and explanations, to which he reverted time and again.

The following year, Theo too finished his schooling, and went to work at the Brussels branch of the Goupil art-gallery. Vincent, however, was transferred to the London branch, leaving to take up his new duties in the middle of May. He knew London already through the works of Dickens, and everything he saw there fascinated him. Coming home from work in the evenings, he strolled along the Thames embankment and made sketches, which he tore up, dissatisfied.

It was in London that Van Gogh had his first unhappy romance, falling deeply in love with his landlady's daughter, Ursula Loyer. But when he asked her to marry him, after walking out with her only a few times, she gave a laughing refusal. This rebuff threw him into such a state of despair that his work began to suffer. His parents had moved once more, this time to the small town of Etten, and when he visited them during his holidays in 1874, his low spirits caused them much concern. He spent all his time drawing. On his return to London that October, he tried to see Ursula again, but in vain.

The winter that followed was a difficult time for Van Gogh. He paid a brief visit to Paris and returned there again in the spring of 1875, when he was transferred to the headquarters of the Goupil art-gallery. His life in the French capital was a lonely one. He had lost none of his passion for painting and visited the Louvre, where he particularly admired Ruisdael's skies and Corot's *Olive Orchard*. He adorned his room with religious engravings and reproductions of Dutch paintings. While he visited the Salon, he does not seem to have had any contact with the impressionist painters.

Just then, however, Van Gogh was primarily preoccupied with religion. He shut himself up in his room for hours on end, to read and discuss the Bible with Harry Gladwell, a young Englishman, who was the only friend he had. At the art-gallery his work now went from bad to worse. He was absent-minded, querulous, and lost his temper with the customers. Suddenly at Christmas-time, he left for Holland without leave, thus coming in for a severe reprimand on his return. After a few more unhappy months, he fled to Etten once more. From there he wrote to Messrs Boussod and Valadon, the directors of the Goupil art-gallery, telling them point-blank that he considered art-dealers to be robbers, detested the business and wished to hand in his resignation.

The atmosphere at Etten was tense. Vincent's moodiness, instability, and even his religious fervor greatly disturbed his family. Theo advised his brother to devote himself to painting, but Vincent was obsessed by his father's example. By chance, he read a newspaper advertisement for the post of French and German master in an English school and, although he had but scant knowledge of either language, his application was accepted and he departed for Kent. Many of the pupils at the establishment where he taught came from poor families. In June the school moved to Isleworth, one of the most wretched of London's suburbs. Van Gogh was sent by his headmaster to collect the school fees from the children's parents. He was appalled by the squalor and misery he witnessed in the course of this errand. Spurred on by his innate sense of pity and by his religious ardor, he finally came to a decision as to his true vocation: he would enter the ministry. He was accepted as a pupil by the Reverend Jones and, although his English was bad and he had not the slightest talent for speaking, he set out to preach to the oppressed and downtrodden. His favorite theme was that sadness and suffering were more valuable than joy and happiness. It is thus small wonder that, far from bringing comfort to his listeners, he only succeeded in disturbing and upsetting them. Van Gogh fell ill and, his nerves completely shattered, returned to Etten at Christmas 1876.

To earn his bread and butter, he worked for a few months as a bookseller's clerk in Dordrecht. There he became increasingly irritable and had violent quarrels with his employer. Moreover his outlandish appearance was bad for business, for his religious aspirations had led him to affect a Quakerish garb.

His family finally agreed to encourage his religious leanings, and he was sent to study at the Protestant Theological Seminary in Amsterdam. His Uncle Johannis, a former shipbuilder, found him a room at the shipyards. But, as Van Gogh had left school at an early age, he needed coaching in Latin and Greek. A teacher, Mr Mendès da Costa, offered to help him, and he set to work with a zeal verging on desperation. But despite fifteen months' hard work, he failed his examinations in July 1878 and was refused admittance to the Seminary.

However, if he could not become a minister, it was still possible for him to preach Christ's gospel as an evangelist. He had heard of a school in Brussels which trained young lay preachers. Training lasted three months, following which he intended to ask for a position in the Borinage (Hainaut Province), a mining-district where conditions were particularly bad. But in Brussels his knowledge of French was considered inadequate. His sermons were at once too direct and too confused.

So even the title of evangelist was refused him. Van Gogh was in despair. His father rushed to Brussels and the Reverend Jones came from England. Following their appeals, he was permitted to go out as a lay preacher to Wasmes.

Amid the squalor and poverty of this primitive community, on which the darkness of the mine seemed to have left its mark, Van Gogh soon began to feel ashamed of being decently dressed and of coming from a land of diligent housewives and carefree children. Discarding even necessities, he wore home-made trousers and a soldier's tunic. He slept in a corner of the hearth, stopped cleaning his house and ceased to wash. In a frenzy of humility, he went from hovel to hovel distributing all he possessed—which was not very much—and spending his nights with sick people whom the doctors had given up. He even cured one of them by his devoted care and power of persuasion. The sight of so much poverty not only moved him to pity but also fired his imagination, and he began to make sketches of women picking coal from the slag-heaps.

The renunciation and self-sacrifice which seemed so natural to him greatly shocked the humble folk around him. They liked him a great deal, but could not think of him as a real minister. The Consistory Inspector, on hearing of the young evangelist's zeal, came to carry out an inspection in the Borinage. He thought that the state of destitution in which Van Gogh was living was exaggerated and in his report spoke of "religious mania." His health shaken by privations and excessive smoking, Vincent fell ill. His landlady, the local baker's wife, notified his family. Pastor Van Gogh immediately came for his son, whom he found lying on a sack filled with straw, shockingly weak and emaciated. He was led off unprotesting by his father, after making the peasants promise to continue holding their religious meetings. And so Van Gogh's career as an evangelist came to an end.

NUENEN

THIS failure precipitated a serious moral crisis in Van Gogh's life. He had betrayed his family's trust and could no longer live in Etten. After a stay with Pastor Pietersen in Brussels, he moved to the small town of Cuesmes in the Borinage. He devoted all his time to drawing, but felt that he stood in need of a teacher. Jules Breton, a second-rate painter whom he admired, lived in Courrières, a mining-town in the north of France. Van Gogh set out to visit him, penniless and on foot, sleeping in barns or in the open air. However, he left Courrières again without daring to knock on Breton's door.

Spring 1880 saw him once more in Etten. There he found a small sum of money left for him by Theo who had moved to Paris, still in the employment of the Goupil art-gallery. Deeply touched by this gesture from his brother with whom he had not corresponded in months, Vincent wrote him a long letter full of remorse for his past failures and also of new hope for the future. Theo's confidence in him was restored and he promised to help him to become a painter. *Letters p 117*

Vincent's hopes of deliverance now centered on art. He knew he had much to learn: the technique of drawing, the laws of perspective, and the use of color. Methodically, he set out to copy Millet's works and tried his hand at large drawings after *The Sower*. But he felt unable to go on working in isolation and accordingly returned to Brussels, "that land of pictures." On Theo's introduction, he became acquainted with Ridder van Rappard, a young aristocrat with a passion for painting.

After a few months thus spent in profitable study and an atmosphere of comparative calm, Van Gogh returned to Etten to see his brother Theo again. But this period of renewed self-confidence and energy was interrupted by a second unhappy love-affair. This time, the object of Van Gogh's affection was his cousin, a young widow and the mother of a little boy. Faithful to her husband's memory, she refused his proposal of marriage. On realizing that she could never be his wife, Van Gogh went to her parents and begged them to let him gaze on her for as long as he could bear the heat of an oil-lamp on his outstretched hand: but he carried this gesture too far and finally collapsed in a faint.

In January 1882 he left for The Hague, where the painters Mauve, Breitner and de Brock were working. He had no difficulty in gaining admittance to their studios, and indeed was welcomed. But the academic art taught even in Mauve's studio disgusted him. One day, in a fit of rage, he broke a plaster-cast and walked out. Subsequently, he picked up Christine (or Sien), a streetwalker, who, first his model, later came to live with him. On this outcast, who was expecting a child by another man, Van Gogh lavished all the pity and tenderness that had been rejected by the women he loved. A celebrated drawing, entitled *Sorrow,* portrays Sien naked and sitting with her head hidden in her hands, a symbol of the tragic destiny of humanity. They lived together as simple working-people in a small studio. In July Sien gave birth to a son in Leyden. To bring in some money, Van Gogh sold a few watercolors, but Sien started drinking again and squandered everything he earned. Pastor Van Gogh paid a visit to his son, bringing him some clothes, and tried to persuade him to leave the girl. But Vincent insisted on staying for the sake of the child. The following winter was a particularly hard one for him, and in June 1883 he fell seriously ill. Theo finally intervened and Vincent decided to break with Sien.

His father was now minister at Nuenen, a village situated in a predominantly Catholic region. Vincent was to remain there for some time, i.e. from December 1883 to November 1885. He organized his life around his work, living in two rooms rented from the verger and working in a washroom which he fitted out as a studio. Two serious blows were still in store for him. One of his neighbors, a sweet-natured but scarcely pretty woman, fell deeply in love with him. Though he did not return her feelings, it was not long before the question of marriage arose. The family intervened to break up the match, and the girl's attempt to commit suicide fortunately miscarried. This was to be the last of his love-affairs. The second blow was even more severe: his father died suddenly on March 27, 1885.

At the beginning of his stay at Nuenen, Van Gogh was well-liked. But his odd ways soon made him an object of general suspicion. Indeed, the village priest finally forbade the members of his flock to sit for him. Alone all day, Van Gogh spent his time thinking, reading, and studying the technical problems set forth in Charles Blanc's *Grammaire des arts du dessin*, a treatise on the fundamental laws of color and the effects obtained by the combination of complementaries on a colored background. Living as he did in a rough, gloomy countryside with overcast skies, Van Gogh still restricted his palette mainly to sepias and bitumens. In his compositions, to which he gave the name of "studies," there was sometimes a bright touch of red or white on a face or a garment, or in the light from a window. He continued to tackle the themes that had always appealed to him: scenes of peasant life, copies Pages 61, 63, 72 after Millet, still lifes of everyday objects, and the rainswept landscapes of Holland. All the experiments of this period are summed up in the large canvas *The Potato Eaters*, which has Pages 65, 67, 68 been spoken of as a forerunner of Expressionism. Van Rappard found the subject of this picture "shocking," and the two friends fell out.

In November 1885, no longer able to endure the stifling atmosphere of Nuenen, Van Gogh decided to go to Antwerp.

where he hoped to sell some paintings. The bustle of the great seaport and his discovery of Rubens came to him like a breath of fresh air. He scoured the antique shops and book-stalls, and in 1886 for the first time came across Japanese prints, which were to influence his work so deeply. After a brief spell at the Karel Verlat studio, he left for Paris, having been told by a friend of the exciting new movements there. In his letters, Theo had already mentioned Impressionism to him.

PARIS

VAN GOGH'S stay in Paris lasted for two years, from February 1886 to February 1888. For the first time he shared his life with Theo, who was in charge of a small art-gallery run by Goupil and Co. The brothers lived together in the Rue Laval, and then at 54 Rue Lepic. After his period of isolation in Nuenen, this companionship was good for Vincent. He enrolled at Cormon's studio, where he worked for four months and where he met Toulouse-Lautrec and Louis Anquetin. Through Theo, he came to know the works of the Impressionist masters—Monet, Renoir, and parti-cularly Pissarro, from whom he learnt the use of bright colors and the art of dividing tones. A little later, at Père Tanguy's well-known shop, he struck up a friendship with Emile Bernard, whom he had previously met casually at Cormon's. Now for the first time Van Gogh was living among painters, accepted as one of them and able to match his works and theories with theirs. He admired the experiments of his friends no less than the great works of Delacroix and Rembrandt which he studied at the Louvre.

Awed by these great examples, he at first drew his inspiration from minor works which he considered to be nearer his own level. His flower-paintings echoed Monticelli's technique, while his urban landscapes were in the style of Raffaëlli. In matters of composition, he was particularly influenced by Japanese wood-block prints of which there was then an excellent collection on view, frequently consulted by painters, at the Bing art-gallery. Pages 87-89

In the late summer of 1886 he became acquainted with Guillaumin, and then with Gauguin, for whom he conceived a deep admiration. A little later he met Seurat, whose *Grande Jatte* had been one of the most remarkable works at the recent Impressionist Exhibition, held in the preceding May and June. Van Gogh's material situation, however, still remained precarious. Neither Theo nor Père Tanguy succeeded in selling a single one of his pictures. He looked round for a suitable place in which he and his friends could display their works. After trying a café, Le Tambourin, run by Segatori, one of Degas' ex-models, he proposed an exhibition in the entrance-hall of the Théâtre Libre. But owing to his violence of manner and unreasonable demands, negotiations soon fell through. He started a group comprising Anquetin, E. Bernard, Lautrec, Signac, Seurat and Gauguin, and a restaurant-proprietor in the Boulevard de Clichy agreed to hang their works in his establishment. However, the customers were scandalized, and the paintings of the "petit boulevard" Impressionists, as Van Gogh wished to call the group in opposition to the Impressionists of the "grand boulevard" featured at Theo's gallery, soon disappeared from the walls.

Van Gogh's enthusiasm was somewhat daunted by the failure of all these schemes, and even Theo's boundless patience with his brother was taxed to the utmost. Van Gogh was so discouraged that he toyed with the idea of a suicide pact with the Scottish painter Alexander Reid, who, as the result of a disappointment in love, also wished to end his life.

In the spring of 1887 Van Gogh recovered his balance to some extent by going with Signac and Emile Bernard on a landscape-painting expedition, in the course of which they joined Seurat on the Island of La Grande Jatte and worked with him there. Also from this period date the two portraits of *Père Tanguy*, a sort of profession of faith in which Van Gogh employed the bright tones of Impressionism in a composition inspired by Japanese prints.

Page 89

After this summer of hard work, Van Gogh watched the winter approaching with dread. It hurt him deeply to have to live at Theo's expense. His health, impaired by under-nourishment as well as by excessive smoking and drinking, went from bad to worse. On Toulouse-Lautrec's advice, he suddenly decided to leave Paris for the South, choosing Arles in Provence, the region of France which he imagined to be most like Japan.

ARLES

HIS fifteen months at Arles (February 20, 1888, to May 8, 1889) were the most significant in Van Gogh's life. The Midi with its violent contrasts of light had a keen appeal for Van Gogh, a northerner and thus more susceptible than most to that yearning for the South which is one of the favorite themes of Nordic literature.

On his arrival at Arles, he took lodgings at the Restaurant Carrel in the Rue de la Cavalerie. The weather was cold and dry, but, attracted by the winter landscape whose clean outlines

Page 35

recalled his native Holland, Van Gogh painted out-of-doors most of the time. He strove to perfect his draftsmanship. In his letters to Emile Bernard, he stressed the necessity of attaining the skill, sureness of touch and mastery of the Japanese. Indeed, when April came and the fruit-trees broke out in snowy blossoms, he might well have believed himself in Japan. Page 93

Towards the middle of May he began to find the Restaurant Carrel too expensive and rented a small studio at 2 Rue Lamar- Page 36 tine. Soon its walls were covered with his new paintings, the various versions of the *Sunflowers*, and fields of iris with blue, Page 95 violet and yellow as the dominant tones.

At the beginning of June he went to Saintes-Maries-de-la-Mer, a place he had long wanted to visit, and it was there that he discovered the Mediterranean and was excited by its changeable colors. Everything in the little town enchanted him. The women there, he said, were as beautiful as figures from Cimabue or Giotto. He rose early in the morning to watch the boats putting out to sea. "Now that I have seen the sea here, I realize that the color must be piled on even more." And he wrote to Theo: "All the colors brought into fashion by Impressionism are changeable; yet one more reason why they should be used boldly; time can only soften them."

His theories about color strengthened, he returned to Arles. It was now summer. "Not the same thing as spring, but I am certainly no less fond of nature, which is beginning to take on a scorched appearance: old gold, bronze, copper, you might call it. With the greenish azure of the sky heated to a white glow, the result is a delightful, utterly harmonious color with broken tones *à la Delacroix*." Fascinated by the dry, flat, stony reaches of La Crau, dotted in the distance with tall, dark cypresses, Van Gogh set to work in a veritable frenzy of creation. Nothing stopped him from painting, not even the fatigue of standing in the fields for hours on end under a hot sun. The night too held him in its spell. With lighted candles encircling his hat, he set up his easel on the banks of the Rhone and painted *Starry Night*. His other great nightscape is *Outdoor Café at Night*.

Pages 70-71
Page 96

In August Van Gogh made the acquaintance of Roulin the postman, who became a close friend as well as a model. During his stay in Arles, he painted an impressive series of portraits: the Roulin family, and Madame Ginoux, "l'Arlésienne."

Page 38

Page 37

Since coming to Provence, Van Gogh had been working at fever pitch. In October Gauguin, who had long intended to join him there but had postponed his trip owing to lack of funds, finally arrived to find his friend worn out by his efforts. Van Gogh complained of headaches and his eyes were giving him trouble. None the less he was extremely happy to have a friend to share his solitude and hoped that his brother Theo would find an easier market for Gauguin's pictures than he had found for his own.

Unfortunately, the two men did not agree on anything and their discussions soon took an acrimonious turn. Gauguin found fault with Van Gogh, for admiring Daumier, Daubigny and Rousseau, and detesting Ingres, Raphael and Degas. Van Gogh's nerves began to give way, and at night he would suddenly find himself standing at Gauguin's bedside for no apparent reason. His behavior became ever more disturbing, like that of a prisoner vainly striving to break down the walls that hemmed him in. After a visit to the Montpellier museum, the two painters had a violent quarrel on the subject of Rembrandt. Finally, on Christmas Eve, the storm broke.

On December 23 Gauguin finished his portrait of Van Gogh painting sunflowers—Vincent and his emblem. That evening, after drinking absinthe, Van Gogh threatened to kill Gauguin, but the latter managed to bring him home and put him to bed. Next morning, ignoring all Van Gogh's apologies, Gauguin decided to return to Paris. Throughout the day the tension mounted. Towards evening Gauguin went out for a breath of air. Hearing "jerky" footsteps behind him, he turned round to find Van Gogh following him like a sleepwalker, a razor in his hand. On being confronted, Van Gogh hesitated a moment and then took flight. Returning to his home, he slashed off part of his left ear. After washing it carefully, he put it in an envelope and took it along to a brothel he sometimes visited. There he asked for it to be given to one of the inmates with the message: "Here is a souvenir from me."

Before setting out on his errand, Van Gogh had staunched the bleeding with towels, bandaged his head, and put on an exceptionally large cap. On returning home, he placed a lighted lamp in his window and retired to bed. Morning found him prostrate on his bed. Outside a crowd had collected at his front-door, for the recipient of the strange gift had aroused the whole neighborhood. Arriving on the scene, Gauguin, who had spent the night elsewhere, was greeted with cries of "What have you done with your friend?", since the bloodstains on the staircase had given rise to the supposition that Van Gogh was dead. Going inside, Gauguin saw that he was only in a deep faint. But at this point, Gauguin's courage failed him and he beat a hasty retreat, taking the next train for Paris. On reviving, Van Gogh was perfectly lucid. He asked after Gauguin and lit his pipe unconcernedly. However, it was thought advisable to take him to St Paul's Hospital, Pages 42, 108, 109 where he found a friend in the person of Dr Rey, who was one of the first to recognize his genius. Under his treatment, Van Gogh's condition rapidly improved and when he wrote to Theo on January 1, 1889, Dr Rey added a few reassuring lines at the end of the letter. On January 7 the painter returned home, but did not start work again until the 21st (*Self-Portrait with Cut* Page 106 *Ear*).

His renewed activity, however, brought with it further attacks of delirium. After a particularly bad attack, which resulted in a petition from the neighbors for his removal, he returned to hospital. In Paris, Theo, who was just about to get married, was full of concern for his brother's welfare and asked the painter Signac to go and see him. Thus it was that Signac spent a day with Van Gogh in the latter part of March; he was to retain the most vivid memory of Van Gogh's stimulating conversation, and was deeply struck by his paintings.

Van Gogh grew weary and resigned. If it was true that he was a danger to others, well, then, it would be best for everyone, and particularly for the peace of mind of Theo and his bride, if he entered a home. His choice fell on the asylum at Saint-Rémy, a small town perched on a hilltop near the "Alpines." He was terrified by the idea of madness, but he thought that, by living among its victims, he might eventually succeed in conquering it.

SAINT-RÉMY

AT the Saint-Rémy Asylum, Van Gogh was kindly received by Dr Peyron, to whom he had been recommended by Dr Rey, and by Mr Salles, a friend of Theo's. He was shown every consideration and given a little room of his own, which he converted into a studio. Unable, however, to endure solitude for very long, he began eating his meals with the other patients and taking an interest in their cases. He was given every opportunity for his work and, in the next year, completed about one hundred canvases and several hundred drawings —this despite three bad attacks, each of which incapacitated him for some time, i.e. from July 6 to the end of August, in December, and from February to April 1890. Although, in the course of his attacks, Van Gogh acted like one possessed, rolling among coal on the floor and swallowing raw paint from the tube, he became completely lucid again as soon as he recovered from the state of complete exhaustion which succeeded them.

Since December 1888, the powers of light and darkness had been battling for possession of his sanity, and he knew it only too well. The spell of madness in the course of which he had attempted to kill Gauguin before doing injury to himself, summed up all the conflicts that had dogged him throughout his life. He felt that he would never be able to live up to the high examples he had set himself: thus his efforts to follow in his father's footsteps by becoming a minister had been doomed to failure; later on, when he became a painter, the works of other artists were a constant reproach to him and he feared that his own were worthless by comparison.

Van Gogh's case has aroused a great deal of interest among psychiatrists, and there has been much speculation as to the exact nature of his mental illness. The general consensus of opinion is that it contained features of both epilepsy and schizophrenia, though of neither in their most extreme forms. While Van Gogh, like an epileptic, experienced attacks of ungovernable rage and hallucinations, generally of a metaphysical or religious nature, he never had an epileptic fit, nor was he to know those moments of euphoria mentioned by Dostoevsky. In his study of the case, Jaspers stressed the pronounced tendency towards schizophrenia and a splitting of the personality. However, Van Gogh never lost his self-awareness, except during his attacks.

Although their themes vary greatly, the paintings of the Saint-Rémy period are closely linked in style, rhythm having replaced color as the artist's main concern. A fresh vision of nature greeted his eyes when, in June 1889, he was permitted to go out to the fields to paint, in the company of a warder. His brush moved in a frenzy of whirling curves, ignoring spatial conventions, uniting earth and sky. And from this tortured formlessness emerged the dark, upward spirals of the cypresses. But he was also attracted by less violent subjects: the garden of the asylum, its flowers and its trees. These he depicted with a delicate attention to detail in which the influence of Japanese prints was once again apparent.

Page 43

Following his attack in December 1889, Van Gogh was very rarely in a fit state to go out-of-doors, though he continued to paint occasional landscapes seen through the bars of his window. As Gauguin had already noticed at Arles, when he said that "quays, bridges, boats—the whole Midi became a second Holland to him," he was still instinctively drawn towards the North. He returned to Millet, his early inspiration, and copied his *Four Hours of the Day* from reproductions, as he had done at the Borinage, but this time in a much more colorful version with a liberal use of yellows and pale blues. In innumerable copies of *The Sower*, the *Raising of Lazarus* after Rembrandt, and the *Prisoners' Round* after Gustave Doré, he succeeded in reconciling his social and religious ideals with his preoccupations as an artist. His homesickness was to come out even more clearly in April 1890, when, on recovering from a bad attack just before leaving for Auvers, he lovingly painted the two versions of *Huts*, so reminiscent of Holland.

Page 112

He was still, however, suffering from acute depression. In January he had learnt of the birth of Theo's son, also called Vincent, and this increased his scruples about living at his brother's expense. He could not even summon up enough energy to write and thank Albert Aurier, who had just published the first article on his work in the *Mercure de France*.

AUVERS

THEO, disturbed by the reports he received on his brother's condition, persuaded Dr Gachet to take Vincent as a private patient. Spring had come to Saint-Rémy, the orchards were in bloom again, and Van Gogh's farewells to the scenes he had been painting were tinged with a certain regret. On May 16 he left for Paris and was met there by Theo on the 17th. The three days he spent in Theo's family circle were gay and happy. Theo's wife was extremely charming and at once took to her brother-in-law. But Vincent found the noise and nervous tension of city-life more intolerable than ever, and was eager to get back to the country. At last, on May 21, 1890, he arrived at Auvers, a small town in the Valmondois region, not far from Paris, near the Isle-Adam.

Dr Gachet had long been interested in art and was a personal friend of painters such as Pissarro and Cézanne. He himself tried his hand at etching, a technique which he was to impart to Van Gogh. The two men liked each other immediately. Gachet at once realized that the best way to calm his patient's troubled spirits was to encourage him to work. Van Gogh stayed first at the Café Saint-Aubin, and subsequently took lodgings at the Café Ravoux in the Place de la Mairie, of which he has left us an impression as innocent and lighthearted as a drawing by a child. At Auvers, as at Saint-Rémy, rhythm was the predominant structural element of his canvases, whose violent brushwork, thick impasto and whirling lines were nevertheless held in check by a strict sense of composition.

Two paintings stand out among the works produced at Auvers: the *Portrait of Dr Gachet* and his last *Self-Portrait*. Page 47 Set against a background of intensest blue, the portrait of the doctor is built around the pale, penetrating eyes with their expression of deep sorrow. The self-portrait in a greenish blue, relieved only by the touch of red in the beard, represents yet one more encounter between Van Gogh and his second self.

Van Gogh's friendship for the doctor, however, soon became charged with mistrust. He fell into violent rages and even threatened the other's life. As Gauguin had done at Arles, Gachet halted his menacing gesture with a single glance.

In June, anxious because his monthly allowance from Theo had failed to arrive, Van Gogh went to Paris for a day. While there, he met Lautrec and Emile Bernard, and was introduced to Aurier. But he did not dare to approach his brother. On his return to Auvers, Dr Gachet, whose duties as railway-doctor took him away from home for a few days each week, was absent. Van Gogh's brain was in a turmoil. He could not bear to be left alone, particularly since he felt his hallucinations returning and no longer had the strength to fight against them. On July 27, 1890, on the pretext that he was going out to shoot crows, he took a revolver and made for the fields. He tried to shoot himself through the heart, but his aim was faulty. Though wounded, he nevertheless mustered sufficient strength to drag himself home. Only a few days earlier, he had painted the same fields, surging and tumultuous, and, above them, the black shapes of crows wheeling in a stormy sky.

Watched over by Dr Gachet's son, Van Gogh spent the night smoking his pipe in a state of complete calm. Although he tried to withhold his brother's address, the latter was notified and came at once. To Theo's plea that he should try to live, Vincent replied: "There'll never be an end to human misery." He died on July 29.

Van Gogh was buried at Auvers-sur-Oise. Theo never recovered from the shock of his brother's death and himself died six months later. His widow had him buried beside Vincent in the graveyard of the little village that had witnessed the painter's last struggles.

FISHERMAN ON THE BEACH, 1882. $(19\frac{1}{2} \times 12\frac{1}{2}'')$
RIJKSMUSEUM KRÖLLER-MÜLLER, OTTERLO, HOLLAND.

THE RESTAURANT, PARIS, 1887. $(17^3/4 \times 21^1/4'')$
RIJKSMUSEUM KRÖLLER-MÜLLER, OTTERLO, HOLLAND.

RESTAURANT CARREL AT ARLES, 1888. $(21^{1}/_{4} \times 25^{1}/_{2}'')$
PRIVATE COLLECTION, U.S.A.

VAN GOGH'S HOUSE AT ARLES, 1888. $(29^7/_8 \times 37'')$
VINCENT VAN GOGH FOUNDATION, AMSTERDAM, HOLLAND.

L'ARLÉSIENNE (MADAME GINOUX), 1888. $(35^{3}/_{8} \times 28^{1}/_{4}'')$
THE METROPOLITAN MUSEUM OF ART, NEW YORK.

THE POSTMAN ROULIN, 1888. $(31\frac{1}{4} \times 25'')$
MUSEUM OF FINE ARTS, BOSTON.

THE TARASCON DILIGENCE, 1888. ($28^{1}/_{4} \times 36^{1}/_{4}"$)
HENRY PEARLMAN COLLECTION, NEW YORK.

SELF-PORTRAIT, 1889. $(18 \times 14^{7}/_{8}'')$
BERNHEIM-JEUNE COLLECTION, PARIS.

VIEW OF ARLES, 1889. $(28^{1}/_{4} \times 36^{1}/_{8}")$
NEUE STAATSGALERIE, MUNICH.

GARDEN OF THE HOSPITAL AT ARLES, 1889. $(28^5/8 \times 36^1/8'')$
DR OSKAR REINHART COLLECTION, WINTERTHUR, SWITZERLAND.

WHEAT FIELD WITH CYPRESSES, 1889. $(28^{1}/_{2} \times 36'')$
BY COURTESY OF THE TRUSTEES, NATIONAL GALLERY, LONDON.

SELF-PORTRAIT, 1889. $(22^{1}/_{2} \times 17^{1}/_{4}'')$
COLLECTION OF MR AND MRS JOHN HAY WHITNEY, NEW YORK.

WHITE ROSES, 1890. $(36\frac{5}{8} \times 28\frac{3}{8}'')$
MRS ALBERT D. LASKER COLLECTION, NEW YORK.

THE CHURCH AT AUVERS, 1890. $(36^1/_2 \times 29^1/_2'')$
BEQUEST OF DR PAUL GACHET, LOUVRE, PARIS.

PORTRAIT OF DR GACHET, 1890. $(26^3/_4 \times 22^1/_2'')$
BEQUEST OF DR PAUL GACHET, LOUVRE, PARIS.

LES VESSENOTS À AUVERS, 1890. ($21\frac{1}{2} \times 25\frac{1}{2}''$)
MRS ROBERT HAHNLOSER COLLECTION, ZURICH, SWITZERLAND.

CHAPTER TWO

THE WORLD OF VAN GOGH

VINCENT THE DUTCHMAN *Chez Etienne*

No better example could be found of a life that became one long aspiration towards the light, a reaching for the stars, than Van Gogh's. In everything he did, he .strove to transcend human realities, to idealize man and hymn his greatness. Take, for instance, his evangelical mission among the miners of the Borinage: its failure was one of the worst blows he ever suffered and yet the motives that led him to devote himself to his fellow men as a preacher were to be the making of him as an artist. Henceforth, he would continue his quest for God through the medium of his painting.

He was not, however, the type of person who withdraws from the world and thinks of God as a kind of mathematical formula. His feet were on the ground, mired in the rich earth in which he was so often to stumble. As far as Van Gogh was concerned, the idealization of man—his painter's way of approaching God—would be inextricably bound up with the misery of human existence. In his works, the most dazzling constellation would always be glimpsed through a cloud of ashes and blood. Thus, through his Christianity, he came to be the herald of expressionism, or rather its prototype.

Van Gogh's case is, however, far from simple, and, despite the exceptional nature of his genius, it would be a mistake to consider him as an isolated figure owing but little to his country or period. All his life he was to remain "Vincent the Dutchman." In other words, by painting reality, often in its grossest and most commonplace aspects, fired by his inner passion, he carried on the art tradition of the Low Countries; and it was in this sense that he continually harked back to Rembrandt. And while he underwent transitory influences, seeking confirmation in painters such as Millet and Delacroix, he was always to preserve the specific qualities of Dutch painting and would never—in this he was no doubt unique—lose touch with his national tradition.

To show his place in that tradition, we have thought it best to quote some strikingly prophetic lines on Dutch art from Eugène Fromentin's *Masters of Past Time* (1876), which still hold good for Van Gogh—who, in fact, had read and re-read them, and they no doubt helped him towards a better understanding of himself.

It was part of the destiny of Holland to be drawn to verisimilitude, to revert to it at some time or another, to live on and find her salvation in the portrait... Dutch painting, one very soon realizes, was not and could not be anything but the portrait of Holland, her outward image, faithful, exact, thorough, life-like, unadorned... The law of its style is to be sincere, its obligation to be truthful. Its first condition is to be familiar, natural, character-revealing; it stems from a concourse of moral qualities—naïveté, patient goodwill and uprightness... Every object, by virtue of the interest it offers, has to be examined in its form and drawn before it is painted... Everywhere we find the same drawing... it seems to spring from everyday observation...

If we look for Rembrandt's ideal in the lofty world of forms, we realize that he saw in it only moral beauties and physical uglinesses... He is more natural than anyone, though not so close to nature, more familiar, though not so earthy, more vulgar and yet quite as noble, ugly in his types...

He had a mania for posing before a mirror and painting himself... but all alone, within a small compass, looking himself in the eyes, intent on himself. Later, after his mature years, fallen on evil days, he comes forward... in dark apparel with a kerchief round his head, his face dispirited, wrinkled, emaciated, his palette in his rough hands.

"He had a mania for posing before a mirror and painting himself..." Like Rembrandt, Van Gogh sought to distinguish between the human and the godlike elements in men's faces, typified by his own—only to find that these are inseparable.

Pages 40, 44, 91, 106

51

HUMAN, ALL TOO HUMAN

UMAN, all too human: this phrase could be used to sum up Van Gogh's career in all its most immediately painful and harrowing aspects. The words moreover imply at once a description of his "case-history" and the final and only possible comment upon it. It might thus seem harsh, and quite uncalled-for, to repeat so essentially cruel a dictum in connection with a painter who was, if anything, pre-eminently human. However in this, the centenary year of Van Gogh's birth, it is perhaps worth considering whether the real truth of the matter does not lie rather in the irresistible sweep, the daring freedom and the glorious certainty of his painting than in the anguish, doubt and appalling suffering of his life. To take his life and describe it in a purely factual way as a sequence of everyday events—there has certainly been no lack of biographers to do so, and life is like that, after all— is to turn it into a long chronicle of failure. From this point of view, the lives of Hölderlin and Nietzsche were also failures, and the same might be said of the sophisticated Proust. Perhaps, indeed, Goethe's social success was an even more serious failure. Be that as it may, the strange frailty that seems to dog all great universal-minded artists through their lives might, on closer scrutiny, be recognized by us as a symptom, the hallmark as it were, of those who are the mediums of total reality and, willy-nilly, must reduce themselves to naught in order to receive it.

But even the most inspired and spontaneous artists have roots somewhere, and Van Gogh's roots were planted in the tough soil of Dutch realism, whose traditions were to weigh heavily on him at the outset of his career, both as a man and as a painter. The Dutch tradition—using the word in its widest historical sense—is a curious mixture of realism and idealism.

1953
see p. 2

In their politics—for example, the revolt of the Dutch "sea-beggars" or the struggles of the Netherlands against Louis XIV in the 17th century—, their religion and their art, the Dutch have always demonstrated a passion for liberty carried to the extremes of social or religious fanaticism, and a practical sense of reality that reveals itself in the sphere of business and also in that of human endeavor. It would certainly be tempting to find a connection between the realism of Dutch painting and the social realism of the Dutch "democracy," thus bearing out Taine's all too famous dictum concerning *"la race, le milieu et le moment."* None the less, in view of the physical, one might almost say geographical, quality of the light in the Low Countries—where, in the vast stretches of plain never far from the sea, only the interplay of light and shadow seems to matter, the drama of chiaroscuro in a setting at once natural and oddly unreal, changing constantly as it does under the buffeting wind—it would seem logical to expect the problem of light to be the major theme of Dutch painting. And, where realism is concerned, surely the knack of minute observation and expressive detail, in a word that sense of expressionism of which we can scarcely fail to detect traces in Rembrandt and Frans Hals, takes its place in the general setting just described.

For expressionism is not simply a way of seeing things: it is also a way of making them, of painting them. An expressionist does not paint "flat" and in pure tones—he breaks up his tones and applies them with a liberal brush. It is striking indeed to find in Rembrandt, Hals, and the Van Gogh of the Nuenen period, the same concern for realism, the same sense of light and feeling for expressive detail, combined with a use of impasto that is no less expressive.

In short, even the most detached and idealistic Dutch painters bear the mark of their national cultural traditions. Vermeer, however abstract, came under the influence of

Caravaggio, that is to say, of realism; and, in our own time, Mondrian's abstractions represent an unusual aesthetic puritanism with a social bias. And Rembrandt's light is the spiritual expression of an observed reality—or at least of such elements of that reality as may be observed.

But such realism, however frank (as in Frans Hals), is not so much concerned to respect the real, the physical aspect of things, as to express it. And while Van Gogh, as a Dutch painter, was certainly deeply attached to reality, his almost religious deference for it was not divorced from painterly considerations. Hence that arbitrary lighting, that no less arbitrary, dramatic and often caricatural distortion—in short, that rugged, uncouth expressionism in which there is nevertheless a glimmer of the total lyrical expression that would later be his. So it is that this essentially lyric painter began by painting the plebeian reality of his time, just as—he must have imagined—Rembrandt and Hals painted the bourgeois reality of theirs. The *Head of an Old Peasant Woman*, painted at Nuenen, Page 63
Pages 65, 67
Page 62
Page 64 and the hands of the *Potato Eaters* thus echo in their crude, awkward way the *Portrait of Margaretha Trip* and the hands of the *Regentessen*.

But Van Gogh had, as it were, mistaken the shadow for the substance, failing to perceive that Rembrandt's realism was in essence illusory. If the Dutch *petits maîtres*, and even more a major figure like the virtuoso Hals, were realists—reproducing, interpreting or stylizing reality—Rembrandt, over and above his subject-matter, was a man obsessed by a light that was not of this world and which he pursued untiringly through the labyrinths of chiaroscuro.

And Van Gogh, fancying himself a social realist, did not as yet realize that it was his mission, and his alone, not simply to mold the recalcitrant clay of reality but to liberate the pent-up inner light of the *Night Watch* and reveal it in all its radiance. Until that moment came, however, he was to languish in the sullen blacks and browns that express the "human, all too human" side of things.

It was this innate taste for reality, moreover—above all, the reality of workers' and peasants' lives—which led him to admire and study the "painters after his own heart," for he had yet to enter on the period of color innovation that was to link him up with other masters. Intuitive by nature and self-taught by inclination and the force of circumstances, Van Gogh always felt impelled to turn to the great painters, regarding them not so much as models in matters of technique as symbolic sponsors of his own experiments. Pages 33, 61, 67, 72, 85

His worship of Millet went deeper than a mere appreciation of his social realism, his predilection for human themes. He was no doubt first attracted by the way in which Millet depicted humble tillers of the soil and so well brought out those essential volumes that were in keeping with this subject. But a study of Van Gogh's various interpretations of Millet's pictures reveals that the all too famous stance of the sower, both realistic and romantic, was no mere literary or melodramatic gesture. For Van Gogh it expressed his own innermost being, his deep yearning for the soil, which he saw as the symbol of reality. Page 111 .Page 66

Later, at Saint-Rémy, when he was repainting his early memories in those vivid colors which he had already borne within him in Holland without being aware of it, he recreated Millet's work in his own image. Page 111

Delacroix was, to his mind, the embodiment of expression in terms of color. Van Gogh had already discovered that master in Holland, and at Arles did not forget him. It is worth noting that, in a letter to Theo (September 8, 1888), he quoted Paul Mantz's comment on the sketch for *Christ on the Lake of Gennesareth*: "I never realized one could get such terrific effects out of blue and green."

Amsterdam, April 3, 1878.

"*By loving steadfastly what is really worthy of love and not wasting it on the insignificant, the empty, the insipid, we gradually acquire more light and, consequently, greater strength.*"

(Letter to Theo)

Laeken, November 15, 1878.

"*As you know, one of the deep-rooted, fundamental truths, not only of the Gospel but of the Bible as a whole, is 'the light that shines in darkness.' Through darkness to light.*"

(Letter to Theo)

THE INNER LIGHT   Charles Estienne

CONSCIOUS to some extent of Delacroix's example, Van Gogh sought to express the upheaval within him in terms of color. True, he may well have had the impossible in mind in asking of color that it should transcend the realities that weigh on the world, and illumine men and things with the incomparable clarity of an inner radiance—but he knew that somehow this light gave meaning to life.

In the Borinage he brooded long over the conditions in which the people there lived, and looked upon the miner's lamp, "intended to guide him through the darkness," as a symbol of man's "faith in God who sees his toil and protects him." Taking his departure from that "darkness which is none the less color" (letter of 1883), he ended up as an "arbitrary colorist" (letter of 1888) intent on expressing "those terrible things, men's passions," thus going from one extreme to the other within the confines of the problem closest to his heart. It was a problem on which his painting, in the course of its development, threw the light his reason could not always provide. For Van Gogh was consumed with the desire to get down to the reality of things, to reflect it in art (since he was a painter) and, finally, to communicate it to his fellow men. Yet the whole social and artistic trend of Dutch tradition led him to confuse this reality with realism. And the reality from which he started—or at least the reality we glimpse in the Nuenen canvases—was all darkness and gloom; we have it in *The Potato Eaters*, a deeply religious work, in which only the lamp suspended above the figures gives a hint of that inner light that was still suppressed, held fast in an ageless, motionless twilight, the eternal dusk of the womb.

Pages 65, 67
Page 68

Nor did abstraction offer a solution; "you find yourself up against a brick wall," he wrote to Emile Bernard in this connection. Reality lay elsewhere. The light he pursued was a purely inner light whose painful emergence is aptly symbolized

Page 69 by that explosion of greenish-yellow light in *The Night Café*, painted at Arles: the lamp above the billiard table, the all but deserted room peopled with drowsy phantoms. And at last,

Pages 70-71 in the human solitude of *The Starry Night* at Saint-Rémy, above the slumbering village, the inner light bursts forth and brims over unimpeded, transcending nature in its reality.

Pages 68-71 In the pages that follow, illustrated by the pictures themselves, we shall see Van Gogh emerging from a fitful light, interwoven with darkness, into an incommensurable clarity of his own creation.

POETRY OF COLOR

The "painter of the future will be a colorist such as there has never been before." This phrase, underlined by Van Gogh in a letter to his brother Theo, is all the more prophetic in that the painter adds: "This will be seen in the generation to follow."

Coming upon Japanese art after his discovery of Delacroix, Van Gogh first regarded color in terms of classical technique, regretting that he had not been taught to handle it sooner. His correspondence is full of comments which, however naïve and over-simple, demonstrate his enthusiasm for color. He urged his brother to send him books on painting "provided that they deal with technique." His first visit to Antwerp brought him a revelation of color that, in its effect upon him, was comparable to the conviction of his evangelical mission. As he had not yet embarked on his great creative phase, he associated tones along traditional lines: "A reddish grey containing relatively little red will appear more or less red according to the colors around it." The Impressionists had already been aware of this, but Van Gogh's conception was quite different from theirs in that he not only approved the use of black (anathema to the Impressionists), but openly maintained that darkness in itself was a color not to be dispensed with, contending, furthermore, that to express form effectively it was preferable to use an almost monochrome color-scheme whose tones differed only in their intensity and values.

More and more frequently, however, he was inspired by a discovery whose possibilities he was, in time, to exploit to the full: *"Color in itself expresses something."* We find him declaring too that, while he had no scruples about borrowing from others, he continued to "see with his own eyes and to conceive things in his own way."

During his stay in Antwerp (1885-1886), Van Gogh also hit upon the rudiments of a system of color symbols not far removed from the technique employed by certain primitive artists who, in their frescos, stained glass and illuminations, attributed special meanings to the various colors. For instance, he was to qualify cobalt as "divine" and carmine as "warm and heady like wine." Perhaps his novel conception of the role of color was to come out most strongly in his moments of crisis. To his way of thinking, all the refinements of traditional technique could not "finish off a picture." "I shall become an arbitrary colorist," he was to say. He would try to "paint infinity" behind a commonplace wall, "to express hope by a star" and "human aspiration by a ray from the setting sun." Emancipating himself from the tones of nature, he would employ "colors suggesting some emotion, warmth, personality." About the same time, he was to speak of expressing "those terrible things, men's passions" in red and green, and repeatedly to assert his fondness for yellow, which he considered as the color of faith, triumph or love. Even the black contour-lines he was to employ were not intended to serve any purely painterly or technical function but to produce "something of a feeling of anguish." He finally concluded that "*exact color* or *exact drawing* could not produce these emotions in themselves."

Van Gogh, then, was to go beyond the traditional idea of painting as an exclusively visual art, thus opening up a wide field of experiment for painters to come. The present-day conception of art as individual creation and self-expression undoubtedly owes much to the idea so clearly expressed by Van Gogh in the following lines: "In life, and in painting too, I can very well dispense with God, but as a man acquainted with suffering, I can't do without something greater than myself, which is my very life: the power to create."

VINCENT VAN GOGH (1853-1890). SNOWY DAY, 1884. $(26^{1}/_{2} \times 49^{1}/_{2}'')$
PRIVATE COLLECTION, DOORN, HOLLAND.

REMBRANDT (1606-1669). PORTRAIT OF MARGARETHA TRIP (DETAIL), ABOUT 1661.
BY COURTESY OF THE TRUSTEES, NATIONAL GALLERY, LONDON.

VINCENT VAN GOGH (1853-1890). HEAD OF AN OLD PEASANT WOMAN, 1885.
(15 × 11¼″) RIJKSMUSEUM KRÖLLER-MÜLLER, OTTERLO, HOLLAND.

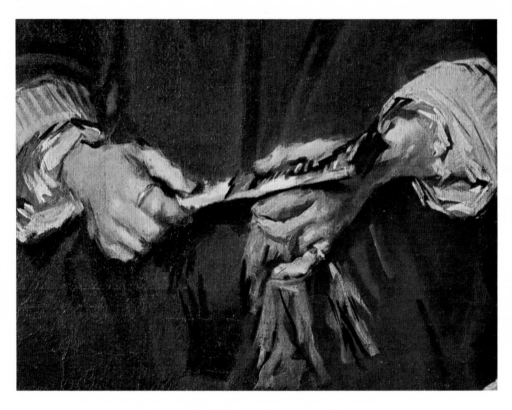

FRANS HALS (ABOUT 1580-1666). THE "REGENTESSEN" OF THE HAARLEM ALMSHOUSE (DETAIL), 1664. FRANS HALS MUSEUM, HAARLEM, HOLLAND.

VINCENT VAN GOGH (1853-1890). THE POTATO EATERS (DETAIL), 1885.
VINCENT VAN GOGH FOUNDATION, AMSTERDAM, HOLLAND.

JEAN-FRANÇOIS MILLET (1814-1875). THE SOWER, 1850. $(40^{1}/_{8} \times 32^{5}/_{8}'')$
MUSEUM OF FINE ARTS, BOSTON.

VINCENT VAN GOGH (1853-1890). THE POTATO EATERS, 1885.
($32^{1}/_{4} \times 44^{7}/_{8}''$) VINCENT VAN GOGH FOUNDATION, AMSTERDAM, HOLLAND.

VINCENT VAN GOGH (1853-1890). THE POTATO EATERS (DETAIL), 1885.
VINCENT VAN GOGH FOUNDATION, AMSTERDAM, HOLLAND.

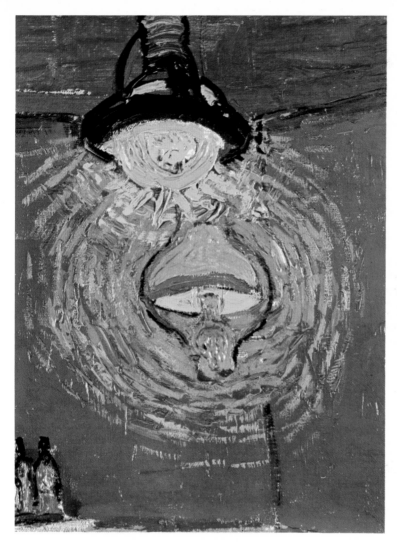

THE NIGHT CAFÉ (DETAIL), 1888. YALE UNIVERSITY ART GALLERY,
NEW HAVEN, CONN. BEQUEST OF STEPHEN C. CLARK.

STARRY NIGHT (DETAIL), 1889. THE MUSEUM OF MODERN ART, NEW YORK.

STARRY NIGHT (DETAIL), 1889. THE MUSEUM OF MODERN ART, NEW YORK.

PEASANT WOMAN SWEEPING, 1885. ($16^{1}/_{8} \times 10^{1}/_{2}''$)
RIJKSMUSEUM KRÖLLER-MÜLLER, OTTERLO, HOLLAND.

CHAPTER THREE

TOWARDS FULFILLMENT

THE PAINTER OF PEASANTS

W HAT was Van Gogh looking for in the desolate, yet picturesque countryside of the Drenthe and at Nuenen, and what did he express there? He gives us the answer in no uncertain terms in one of his letters, writing: *"When I say I*

Pages 33, 61, 63, 67, 72

am a painter of peasants it is the literal truth and you will see later that I feel most at home among them. It's not for nothing that I have spent so many evenings brooding before the fire in the homes of miners,

Page 85

turfcutters and weavers."

At the outset of his career, Van Gogh took up a position that was new in Dutch art. "In the old pictures, the people didn't work," he remarked; "at present I'm sweating over a picture of a woman I saw this winter pulling up carrots in the snow." And by painting such "impossible" subjects as old shoes or a heap of potatoes, he made his position even clearer. He painted peasants, working people and their everyday environment just as he found them, since in his opinion there was greater dignity in the simple life of the Dutch countryside than in the superficial glitter of the towns. And so he celebrated the humble villages, the peasants wresting a precarious livelihood from the muddy fields, tilling the soil in which they would one day be buried; he celebrated man attached to the land from time immemorial, indeed condemned to it, awaiting the coming of God with resignation. He painted their misery with the same vehemence and passion he had put into his evangelical work among them. As a matter of fact he was never destined to know any other type of humanity. Dutch or French, inhabitants of Nuenen or Arles, the faces and hands he painted were always those of the people.

THE letters written while he was still in Holland prove that Van Gogh was wrestling with the problem of color even before he went to Paris and came into contact with the Impressionists. Thus we find him describing the northern landscape in much the same way he was later to paint those of Arles and Saint-Rémy.

Pages 41, 43, 93, 94, 110

Amsterdam, November 1883.

In the moss, green-golden tones, on the ground, a dark mauve-grey verging on red, blue or yellow, tones of an inexpressible purity...

An untainted, luminous sky, not white, but of a mauve defying analysis, white with red, blue and yellow running into it, a sky that reflects everything and of whose presence you are everywhere aware, a hazy sky in harmony with the light mist below.

Nuenen, October 1885.

Red ochre forming orange with yellow ochre, their combination with blue is more neutral, and so they become either more red or more yellow in relation to this neutralized color. The strongest light in the whole of this canvas is simply pure yellow ochre. And the fact that this muffled yellow still tells out well is because it lies in a broad field of a kind of almost neutral violet, red ochre combined with blue yielding violet tones.

Nuenen, October 1885.

Color in itself expresses something, it cannot be dispensed with and must be turned to good account; whatever is beautiful, truly beautiful, is also true.

75

PARIS AND EARLY MONTHS AT ARLES

THE aesthetic phenomenon of Impressionism is decidedly an ambiguous one. At first sight, it may seem to be just another movement in art, taking its rise at a given moment in history, the more so as it appears to link up with Chevreul's theories of color. But if we examine it more closely and ask ourselves why an artist who was not impressionist—Van Gogh for instance—should nevertheless be drawn towards the movement at a certain stage of his development, the question arises as to whether Impressionism does not in fact represent an organic tendency, a deep-rooted need in art, rather than a movement or a group—in other words, a sort of spring-time regeneration, purging blood and spirit of the dross and "melancholy humors" of the winter. Impressionism certainly provided such a regeneration, a refreshing immersion in nature which brought painting a renewed awareness of such things as purity of sensation and touch.

Van Gogh, no doubt, vaguely hoped to find in Impressionism, and also in the atmosphere of Paris, the vital, authentic contact with reality that had finally been denied him at Nuenen in the black country. In fact the Impressionists themselves were convinced that they were being realists, as opposed to the idealism of the academic studios, whereas in actual practice they brought into being an art of pure imagination: an art which in the eyes of the public, who was not "taken in," was totally and indeed flagrantly unreal. It was only much later that the why and wherefore of this game of hide-and-seek between idealism and realism was to be understood, and the discovery made, as if by magic, of the exact artistic point at which the painter's ideal and his image of the real inevitably merge into the natural, poetic act of painting. But in 1887 that moment had not yet arrived.

There is a strange idea, which is still current, to the effect that color flourishes in sunny lands and, moreover, that the South of France is the very birthplace and home of color. On the strength of this misconception, it has long been found perfectly natural and fitting that Van Gogh's most daring and decisive experiments in color should have been made in the Midi, as was also to be the case with those of Bonnard, Matisse, Chagall and Miro.

But such an assumption ignores the obvious fact that the sun in itself is not color. It is perhaps—indeed there can be no doubt about it—the soul of color, but in it all color is lost and dissolved. The sun-drenched countries are not in the least colorful—quite the contrary, in fact. The slightest familiarity with the Mediterranean landscape, and particularly with that of Provence, bears this out: unrelievedly ashen and dusty, all greys, pale greens and silvers. The sun is the very symbol of life; nevertheless, in many respects, Greece, Provence, Spain and Africa strike us as being strangely funereal, and this impression is not belied by Spanish or Negro art.

Color, pure color, is a prismatic effect derived from atmospheric refraction. There is no need to be a scientist to realize that the best, the most natural prism is a more or less humid atmosphere. This simple fact explains why such regions as Normandy and the Ile-de-France, rather than the Midi, gave birth to Impressionism.

Pure color implies full tones, "unbroken" by mixtures, by those greys and shadings which effect transitions in a composition. In time critics came to speak of a "patchwork of color" in a derogatory sense to characterize not only the decorative art of the East, and Western folk art, but also the most barbaric and objectionable features of modern art.

Now this colorful idiom serving for expression as well as decoration is a phenomenon coming from the North, West or East, but rarely or never from the Mediterranean. Going beyond—or rather harking back from—Impressionism, it is not concerned with optical data based on more or less scientific observation. Its origin lies in a remoter, almost immemorial folk tradition: a color-scheme is discovered, or rediscovered, which is the very creation of the artist, needs no theories to justify it, is a world in itself and, in the last analysis, seems much more a product of the painter's inner "sun"—his life force, his power of imagination—than of the other sun that blazes in the sky above him.

There is nothing fanciful in this explanation, based as it is on the simplest facts of ethnography, the psychology of primitive peoples and children, and the paintings of some typical colorists. Where, for example, did Gauguin have his revelation of total color? The answer is in Brittany, and *La Belle Angèle* in her traditional costume is as highly colored as a totem-pole. Van Gogh's case is more complex, but the solution is not hard to find if we consider that, as a Dutchman, a Northerner, he must have been unconsciously influenced—all question of tulip-fields apart—by the extraordinarily vivid colors of certain Dutch traditional costumes. The same colors were to be discovered in Holland twenty years later by Kandinsky, who had already observed them on traditional costumes elsewhere in 1889, in the course of an ethnographical mission to northern Russia. "I felt," he wrote at the time, "as though I had wandered into a painting."

The exciting thing about all this is that for Kandinsky, as for Van Gogh, the decisive revelation where painting was concerned was French Impressionism. In the case of the Russian painter it was a Monet exhibited in Moscow about 1900 that first made him aware of "the superhuman power of colors in themselves"—a phrase that pays its respects to Impressionism and at the same time goes considerably beyond it. And this link between Kandinsky's quasi-oriental art and the course of modern painting can only serve to increase our understanding of Van Gogh's lifelong passion for Japanese art, a passion that bordered on the fanatic.

Thus "Japan in Provence" did not mean that the Provençal landscape had merely needed the impress of a certain stamp of mind to become Japanese; while it is impossible now to think of certain parts of Doubs, the Ile-de-France and Brittany without recalling Courbet, Monet and Gauguin, Provence is no more Japanese after Van Gogh than it was before. Nevertheless, if it is not Japanese, certain forms and features—the contorted gestures of the olive-trees, the unkempt slopes of the motionless "Alpines"—bear the mark of Van Gogh for all time. In other words, Japan did not merely provide him with a lesson in pictorial method and artistic freedom, but represented for him what Jean Leymarie has called his "Orient": a semi-fabulous, semi-real country, absolved from the burdens and taint of material things, a country in whose vast, illusory distances only what is most free and dazzling remains, the marvelous world of color and rhythm, together with the key to its secret. A modern primitive, Van Gogh certainly carried this world within himself, but at the outset of his career he probably saw painting in too serious a light and associated it too much with a social conscience to be able to express himself in terms that seem more appropriate to children and savages. Japanese art is direct proof that a world of rhythm and color exists in its own right, and it was Japan that, at one bound, released his extraordinary lyrical gift, his genius for the unreal—if, after all, such a term can be applied to Van Gogh's or to any human experience. He knew reality at first hand, but abandoned the outward, seeming link of events and anecdotes with life in favor of an inner rhythm, the music of solitude, the rhythm of the world.

To accept this rhythm, to exalt man's kinship with the sun, to set such a high price on human dignity and happiness as to take the risk of being utterly consumed in the process, immolating oneself as it were for the salvation of all—such was Van Gogh's overwhelming achievement, already apparent in the work of the first few months at Arles. Wherein lies the particular fascination of the yellows, blues and reds of that fabulous springtime so quickly maturing to summer? What makes this painting so much more human than that of his Nuenen period? The feeling of impending disaster? No—rather a vast, heroic aspiration towards happiness, mingled with an awareness of the sun, the life-force behind all human striving. And it is in this sense that Van Gogh was a truly social painter.

However, the arbitrary procedures of Monet and Renoir were far from being as radical as Van Gogh's unrealistic approach. What the latter was after was *light* itself, which is inimitable, is not encountered casually, has nothing to do with clouds and skies; if it is relative to anything, it is not to the external world, but to the painter himself. In other words, it is an absolute. Van Gogh was so constituted that he could not aspire to or achieve any reality other than his own. Moreover, in the course of his impressionist experiments in Paris he had already studied and practiced Japanese line and lay-out. In the Page 91 1887 self-portrait, the face is set against a whirling background, whose concentric movement owes nothing to Impressionism. So it was with Seurat, round about the same time, as regards divisionism; he recast reality in the same high-handed fashion. And, going even farther it may be noted that the static, hide-bound Seurat occasionally (as in *La Poudreuse*) allowed himself to indulge in rapid, circular brushwork of a type completely unexpected in his work. This may be sheer coincidence. Nevertheless, Seurat was the last painter visited in Paris by Van Gogh before his departure for Arles.

To his contemporaries, there was nothing unreasonable
or mysterious in a taste for Japanese art. Degas, Manet and
Monet, for example, found in it what they sought in Impressionism, namely an exact and spontaneous feeling for nature,
to which was added an extraordinary precision of composition
and line that prevented this feeling from becoming vague
and formless. In the next generation, Gauguin and Lautrec
—and, later on, Bonnard and Vuillard—invoked Japanese art
for almost the opposite reasons. It was their desire to go
beyond Impressionism, and in their works such features as
arabesques, flat surfaces, contour-lines and two-dimensional
space—in short the stock-in-trade of the abstract in painting—
became the pictorial elements of an exciting interplay between
modern Western art and the art of the Far East.

Van Gogh proceeded differently. First of all, there was
his breathtaking handling of space, those amazing recessions
which, in the most impressive of the Arles and Auvers landscapes, sweep the eye from foreground to background along
a broad arc that leaps towards the vanishing point. Such effects,
delineated with a masterly lightness of touch, he found ready
to hand in the Japanese landscape, whose practitioners had
always delighted in visual paradoxes, at once hollowing and
flattening, suggesting depth and, at the same time, reducing
it to calligraphic symbols. Unusual for Van Gogh is the delicate
handling of the *Pont d'Asnières* of his Paris period, in which
the scene is barely described, merely suggested with the tip
of the brush, "written in" as it were, quite in the Japanese
manner. But there was, to be sure, more to it than that. In
Japanese prints he had certainly seen what others had seen
and had benefited from it: flat tones, arabesques and, in this
case, two-dimensional space, a space which would appear to
be more decorative than expressive, but which he nevertheless
made the basis of his expression. And in them, he discovered

Pages 41, 43, 48, 93

Page 88

above all what Gauguin termed the "right to dare everything," not merely in the sense of technical freedom, but in a moral sense as well. This qualification is not too strong, if we consider the incredible contrast—night and day—between the muted

Page 95 colors of Nuenen and the solar blaze of the *Sunflowers* at Arles. What had occurred was in the nature of a rebirth, the emergence of a whole human being, and, looking back from

Page 89
Page 34 the Arles period to the portrait of *Père Tanguy* (1886) and the flower-filled *Restaurant* (1887), more like a Japanese spring than a pointillist or neo-impressionist painting, we can see whence Vincent the Dutchman gained the courage to "dare everything"—in other words, to throw overboard all moral and family constraints, an oppressive pictorial tradition, and a seeming reality that did not reflect his image or, if it did, reflected it in the most drab and lifeless way.

FULFILLMENT — *Charles Estienne*

U<small>NDER</small> the burning August sky of Arles, Van Gogh was
at last to <u>reap</u> the full fruits of his genius and enjoy
a brief <u>harv</u>est of creative plenty and fulfillment. While his
life is usually divided into a number of periods corresponding
more or less automatically to the high points of his art, his
departure from Paris did not immediately mark any development
in his style. Between his impressionist treatment of the Parisian
spring and the delicate snows and blossoms of the first few
months at Arles, there is little to choose. His search for "Japan
in Provence" led him back to the same source: the visionary
light, the inner sun of the painter.

However, from August onwards, in the "gloriously strong,
windless heat" of that spellbound, motionless summer, a
change became apparent. And, as summer reached its peak,
and the high noon of the year brought with it that gleaming
sense of fulfillment and expansion in man and nature for which
another poet of the sun, René Char, was later to coin the
expressive term "Augustness," Van Gogh left his earlier
achievements behind, cut himself off from them and seemed
at last about to realize his old dreams of communion with
his fellow men and with reality, this time in the form of "nature
become extraordinarily beautiful."

And thus, in the blaze of August, Van Gogh found fulfillment. He was now in the very center of his world of light,
and his inner radiance, symbolized by that enigmatic lamp   Page 69
which kept cropping up in his pictures, was also the radiance
of the sun—and of the far-flung stars. For, if August with its
"high yellow note" ushered in the triumph of day, September
brought him the soothing depths of space and the infinite
possibilities of night. The yellow was still there in the shim-
mering of the stars in the distance, the halo of candlelight   Pages 70, 71

playing round the painter's hat, the light breaking over figures and objects—but night was also present in the singing richness of a blue unique in Van Gogh's work.

This starlit blue—as his letters of the previous month indicate—was, at least in the beginning, a symbol of hope. It was not long, however, before his elation vanished and depression took its place. After experiencing a tension and relaxation which were equally profitable, Van Gogh found this period of almost unnatural calm and temporary self-release giving way to one of further tension, and sensed another hour of judgment looming ahead. The sinister *Night Café* undoubtedly belongs to this period of transition: the harmonies of yellow and blue have disappeared and are replaced by cold yellows and a shrill combination of red and green, which was to become even more strident later on in *Gauguin's Armchair* and the *Self-Portrait with Cut Ear*.

September came to an end, the harvest was gathered in and once more the earth lay bare. Before another month had passed, Gauguin would be there. Two opposing planets would meet and clash, obeying both in their attraction and impact a law akin to that of the elemental forces of nature. Gauguin embodied the forces of order and measure, the window on the natural world, the balance inherent in earth and water. In Van Gogh, born of the earth but violently ripped away from it, we find the forces of excess, instability and an aggressiveness that was turned even against itself. He was to realize himself only by self-destruction, by dissolving into fire and air, into the world of those strange symbols whose significance transcends their artistic function—the giant disc of the sun and the flaming sword of the cypresses.

But beforehand, he had to meet his opposite number, a man whose personality embodied so much that he admired and could never be: his fellow painter, his friend Gauguin.

THE LOOM, 1884. $(27^1/_2 \times 33^3/_8'')$
RIJKSMUSEUM KRÖLLER-MÜLLER, OTTERLO, HOLLAND.

STILL LIFE, 1884-1885. $(18^{1}/_{4} \times 22'')$
H. P. BREMMER COLLECTION, THE HAGUE, HOLLAND.

A CORNER OF MONTMARTRE, PARIS, ABOUT 1886. $(13^{3}/_{4} \times 25^{1}/_{4}'')$
VINCENT VAN GOGH FOUNDATION, AMSTERDAM, HOLLAND.

LE PONT D'ASNIÈRES, 1886-1887. ($21^{1}/_{2} \times 18''$)
COLLECTION OF MR AND MRS F. H. HIRSHLAND, HARRISON, N.Y.

LE PÈRE TANGUY, ABOUT 1886. $(36^1/_8 \times 28^3/_4'')$
MUSÉE RODIN, PARIS.

STILL LIFE WITH BOOKS, ABOUT 1886. $(20^3/_4 \times 28^1/_2'')$
VINCENT VAN GOGH FOUNDATION, AMSTERDAM, HOLLAND.

SELF-PORTRAIT, 1887. $(17^1/_4 \times 14^3/_4'')$
VINCENT VAN GOGH FOUNDATION, AMSTERDAM, HOLLAND.

LA MOUSMÉ, 1888. $(28^3/_4 \times 23^3/_4'')$ CHESTER DALE COLLECTION,
NATIONAL GALLERY OF ART, WASHINGTON, D.C.

ORCHARD IN BLOOM, 1888. $(11^{3}/_{8} \times 14^{1}/_{2}'')$
H. P. BREMMER COLLECTION, THE HAGUE, HOLLAND.

LE PONT DE L'ANGLOIS, ARLES, 1888. $(23^{1}/_{8} \times 24^{1}/_{4}'')$
PRIVATE COLLECTION.

SUNFLOWERS, 1888. $(37^{1}/4 \times 28^{3}/4'')$
VINCENT VAN GOGH FOUNDATION, AMSTERDAM, HOLLAND.

OUTDOOR CAFÉ AT NIGHT, 1888. $(31 \times 24^{3}/_{4}'')$
RIJKSMUSEUM KRÖLLER-MÜLLER, OTTERLO, HOLLAND.

FROM THE SYMBOL TO SPACE

ROM the miner's lamp of Nuenen to the one he placed on his window-sill following the scene with Gauguin; from the evening star he noted in 1875 in Corot's *Olive Orchard* to the letter he wrote to his brother in August 1888, in which he said: "Some day or other you will see a picture of the little house itself bathed in sunlight, or else with the window lighted and a starry sky above"—throughout these years Van Gogh was obsessed by the symbolism of luminous objects and of color. The lamp was a symbol of calm and security. The star symbolized faith, and gaslight, human realities. Deep ultramarine blue was infinity, while red and green expressed "those terrible things, men's passions." Page 36

Prior to August 1888, he revealed these ideas only in his letters and made no real attempt to apply them in painting. There is no trace of them in the works of Holland and Paris, nor in the canvases he produced at Arles between February and August 1888 (*Orchard in Bloom*, *Le Pont de l'Anglois*, *Boats* Pages 93-94 *at Saintes-Maries*, and many others), which are impressionist, "Japanese," decorative rather than expressionist and, in short, similar to those he had been painting in Paris.

Two letters dated August and September 1888 throw a special light on Van Gogh's intentions. In August, he asserted his determination to become an "arbitrary colorist" so that he might paint the portrait of an artist friend "who dreams great dreams." In his picture he wished to express "his appre-   Page 103 ciation and love for him"; the fair head set against a background of rich blue would "produce a mysterious effect like a star in the azure depths of the sky." In the second of these letters, he spoke of his house at Arles, the lighted window and the starry sky above: a strange premonition of the scene with Gauguin. And yet Gauguin was not a mere harbinger of catastrophe, or even an innocent symbol of it. On the contrary, he came with a precious gift which was not to be lost on Van Gogh: that virile feeling for plastic values, that keen sense of construction in terms of color which imparted a last degree of strength and solidity to the great symbolic pictures of Van Gogh's closing cycle of works.

Charles Estienne

THE LAST PHASE

"In an artist's life, death is perhaps not the most difficult thing."

H OWEVER paradoxical and even shocking it may be, the truth is that with Van Gogh we have a great painter whose art seems to bear little relation to the actual circumstances of his life—or even to those of his death. Only a few of the seventy pictures and thirty-two drawings made at Auvers-sur-Oise—his supreme period "of a productivity unparalleled in any artist's career"—contain any direct intimation of the approaching disaster: the two cornfields (*In Storm* and *With Crows*), the blue and green self-portrait of May 1890 (terrifying in its very calm) and one or two landscapes in which the cottages are no longer those of France, but rise from the northern plains, from Groot Zundert where Van Gogh spent his earliest childhood—the merest hint that the wheel had nearly come full circle.

Page 112

At times these last pictures are curiously like those Van Gogh painted at Paris and Arles in the spring of 1888. There is a quality in them, not exactly of joy but of extraordinary freshness and freedom from tension, marvelously expressed by blues, greens and purples with occasional pinks and a few brilliant notes of red. Over-emphatic symbols were progressively disappearing from the painter's work: "I have kept (from Saint-Rémy)," he wrote to Gauguin, "a cypress with a star, a last attempt—a star softly glowing in pink and green." Above all, these pictures contain an overwhelming aspiration towards rest and peace that has, however, nothing morbid about it: "I should like to paint portraits against a very bright yet restful background. Greens of different qualities but of the same value, forming an over-all green that in its vibration would recall the soft rustling of ripe corn."

AFTER VAN GOGH

VAN GOGH's direct successors, at least from the technical standpoint, were of course the Fauves. And one of the significant turning-points in the history of modern painting was the meeting of Matisse, Vlaminck and Derain at the opening of the Van Gogh exhibition at Bernheim-Jeune's in March 1901. It was on this occasion that Vlaminck exclaimed: "I love Van Gogh better than my own father!"

This, it will be noted at once, is an emotional rather than an aesthetic reaction. And we may well ask ourselves, in fact, whether Van Gogh's use of color would really have had the "effect of a thunderbolt" on the young Fauves-to-be, if it had offered no more than a new, highly stylized brushwork in which the picture surface came to life with color applied straight from the tube, and if it had not been charged with intense feeling, endowed with an almost superhuman power of expression. The answer is not far to seek and, even taking into account the remarkable similarities between the style and spirit of Van Gogh's procedures and the practices of the Fauves at the outset of the movement, it becomes obvious that the influence of the painter of Arles and Auvers is not to be looked for on this purely technical level.

For the problem, one which haunted Van Gogh throughout his career, was precisely that of transcending the purely physical and technical limitations of painting. It was a problem that called for a restatement—and even today continues to do so—of the very bases of art itself, or at least as normally practiced within the bounds of its specific expressive means and particularly of the feelings and sensations which it normally arouses. Thus we see why Matisse—with his usual wisdom, which never deserted him even at the height of Fauvism— owed but little to Van Gogh, whose undisguised vehemence and tense spiritual aspirations, not to mention his obsession with the sun and with sunflowers, were a far cry from his own experiments in abstraction, carried out with such equanimity and unruffled peace of mind.

Vlaminck himself, who came closest of all to Van Gogh during his early period at Chatou, when his colors were still Page 113 swirling to an elemental rhythm—he, too, was soon to turn into quieter paths. Another point to be remembered here is that the responsibility for liberating color—or rather liberating painting by means of color—cannot be attributed to Van Gogh alone. Gauguin also played a key part, and this fact throws much light on the smoldering antagonism between the two painters. The work of both led up inevitably to the crucial shifting of emphasis that made itself felt, from art *per se* to its power of expression: expression at any price, even at the expense of its own integrity and its seeming *raison d'être*.

Van Gogh's impact and the rift it produced can perhaps best be understood by following the line of deviation down to Picasso's *Weeping Woman,* a bombshell that is emotional Page 116 rather than baroque, a blast of expression rather than a statement of aesthetic values.

That line had previously passed by way of Soutine, though the latter claimed to have no particular sympathy for Van Gogh's work. This is beside the point. It is enough to recall the feverishly whirling curves of his Cagnes and Céret landscapes to detect the presence, involuntary or unavowed, of one of the most violent features of his precursor's work. But there are even surer indications, the more convincing for being less obvious, in the spiritual and artistic kinship that links these two still lifes by Van Gogh and Soutine—one with barely Pages 114-115 a trace of color and the other to all intents and purposes in monochrome—with a tradition of which Rembrandt is both the master and the symbol. To sound the depths of light and shadow, to locate man within them, to express in paint his soul and conscience—such was the passion and the triumph shared in common by Rembrandt, Van Gogh and Soutine.

That we can go directly on from this point to Picasso's resounding break with the past is a fact that makes Van Gogh loom large indeed in the immediate background of present-day art; for after him there came not only the Fauves, but the whole spirit of modern expression.

PORTRAIT OF THE BELGIAN PAINTER EUGENE BOCH, 1888. $(23^1/_2 \times 17^5/_8'')$
LOUVRE, PARIS.

103

GAUGUIN'S ARMCHAIR, 1888. $(35^{1}/_{4} \times 28^{1}/_{4}'')$
VINCENT VAN GOGH FOUNDATION, AMSTERDAM, HOLLAND.

THE NIGHT CAFÉ, 1888. $(27^1/2 \times 35'')$
YALE UNIVERSITY ART GALLERY, NEW HAVEN, CONN.
BEQUEST OF STEPHEN C. CLARK.

SELF-PORTRAIT WITH CUT EAR, 1889. $(20 \times 17\frac{5}{8}'')$
COLLECTION OF MR AND MRS LEIGH B. BLOCK, CHICAGO.

106

VAN GOGH'S BEDROOM AT ARLES, 1889. $(28^{1}/_{4} \times 35^{3}/_{4}{''})$
VINCENT VAN GOGH FOUNDATION, AMSTERDAM, HOLLAND.

THE HOSPITAL AT ARLES, 1889. (29 × 36⅛″)
DR OSKAR REINHART COLLECTION, WINTERTHUR, SWITZERLAND.

PORTRAIT OF THE SUPERINTENDENT OF ST PAUL'S HOSPITAL, 1889.
(24 × 18″) MADAME G. DÜBI-MÜLLER COLLECTION, SOLOTHURN, SWITZERLAND.

THE OLIVE ORCHARD, 1889. $(27^7/8 \times 35^1/4'')$
RIJKSMUSEUM KRÖLLER-MÜLLER, OTTERLO, HOLLAND.

PEASANT BINDING WHEAT INTO SHEAVES (AFTER MILLET), 1889.
($17^{1}/_{4} \times 12^{3}/_{4}$″) VINCENT VAN GOGH FOUNDATION, AMSTERDAM, HOLLAND.

VINCENT VAN GOGH (1853-1890). HUTS (SOUVENIR OF THE NORTH), 1890.
($17^7/8 \times 16^7/8$") PRIVATE COLLECTION, THE HAGUE, HOLLAND.

MAURICE VLAMINCK (1876-1958). HOUSE IN THE COUNTRY, 1906.
($21^{1}/_{4} \times 25^{1}/_{2}$") PRIVATE COLLECTION, PARIS.

CHAÏM SOUTINE (1894-1943). HERRINGS, 1916. $(25^{1}/_{2} \times 19^{1}/_{2}'')$
KATIA GRANOFF COLLECTION, PARIS.

VINCENT VAN GOGH (1853-1890). STILL LIFE WITH MACKEREL, 1886-1887. $(14^{3}/_{4} \times 21^{5}/_{8}")$ DR OSKAR REINHART COLLECTION, WINTERTHUR, SWITZERLAND.

PABLO PICASSO (1881). WOMAN WEEPING, 1937. $(23^{1}/_{2} \times 19^{1}/_{2}")$
SIR ROLAND PENROSE COLLECTION, LONDON.

NOTES ON THE PLATES
SELECT BIBLIOGRAPHY
EXHIBITIONS
LIST OF COLOR PLATES
INDEX OF NAMES

NOTES ON THE PLATES

PAGE 85: THE LOOM, 1884.

At Nuenen Van Gogh had often observed the weavers with their "dreamy, pensive, almost somnambulistic appearance" and their precise, practiced gestures as they went about their work amid the complicated framework of their looms. He took pleasure in painting them, almost swallowed up as they were in the scaffolding of dark, rough-hewn wood. We may note, however, that the will to realism and the concern for depicting an artisan at his daily task have almost completely slipped into the background, tempted away as the artist was by the loom's fascinating, abstract maze of lines—the real subject of the picture rather than the loom itself.

PAGE 86: STILL LIFE, 1884-1885. *Bottle & jugs*

In this work, done to all intents and purposes in monochrome on a theme that can hardly be called inspiring, Van Gogh succeeded in producing a painting remarkable not only for its satisfying texture but for the harmonic balance with which the volumes have been distributed under the light. What an exercise of skill this weaver and these bottles were for such a draftsman as he! In its utter simplicity, this picture deliberately tackles and solves a quite different problem from that of *The Loom*, which is an almost two-dimensional composition. Here, on the other hand, we find a homage to chiaroscuro, humbly but masterfully paid.

PAGE 87: A CORNER OF MONTMARTRE, PARIS, ABOUT 1886.
PAGE 88: LE PONT D'ASNIÈRES, 1886-1887.

It is a known fact that Far-Eastern painting, and particularly that of the Japanese, is an art of highly expert calligraphers. Thus we may say that few of Van Gogh's works are as oriental, i.e. as "calligraphic," as this *Pont d'Asnières*. For lightness of touch and discretion of effect it bears comparison with the most graceful landscapes of the Japanese masters. It seems obvious that Van Gogh's brushwork, intricate and tortured as it often is, takes its rise—or at least its cue—from the calligraphy of such painters as Hokusai and Hiroshige. In a wholly different vein is this *Corner of Montmartre*, whose lively sparkle and freshness reflect an Orient of pure imagination.

PAGE 90: STILL LIFE WITH BOOKS, ABOUT 1886.

This still life may well be a symbol of that cultured background for which Van Gogh, a voracious reader, always yearned. Yet we cannot fail to see that, even when the theme is a mere pile of books, Van Gogh's rendering borders on the abstract.

PAGE 92: LA MOUSMÉ, 1888.
PAGE 93: ORCHARD IN BLOOM, 1888.

We find a noticeable Japanese influence both in this colorful orchard and in the Mousmé—i.e. a Japanese girl—whose title was suggested to Van Gogh by a novel of Pierre Loti, *Madame Chrysanthème*.

PAGE 104: GAUGUIN'S ARMCHAIR, 1888.
PAGE 106: SELF-PORTRAIT WITH CUT EAR, 1889.

Gauguin's Armchair and the *Self-Portrait with Cut Ear*: few of Van Gogh's pictures are as steeped in the symbolic as these. We may note, however, that the symbols—the gas flame, the candle, the pipe, the wound—are treated with a true painterly concern for the picture surface and a harmonious division of its area.

PAGE 107: VAN GOGH'S BEDROOM AT ARLES, 1889.
PAGE 108: THE HOSPITAL AT ARLES, 1889.

Now the symbols are relegated to the background (both psychologically and pictorially speaking), or rather are just where they should be, for here Van Gogh was intent on organizing space, on building up the picture in terms of color. Despite appearances, and without sacrificing any of his personality, he perhaps never again so closely approached that total abstraction which, if not an end in itself, is the very syntax of the painter's art. Fine, powerful expressionist though he is, Van Gogh described this picture of his bedroom in terms of an undisguised symbolism that curiously links him with the Fauvism of Matisse. "This time it's my bedroom," he wrote in a letter to Theo; "color alone has to put the thing across, its simplification imparting a grander style to the work and hinting at rest and sleep generally. The sight of this picture is meant to relax the mind, or rather the imagination." This puts it perfectly. And his deep desire for plastic (and indeed for physical) harmony embraces its object, surprisingly enough, in passages which, overwrought though they are, seem to express an almost wistful delicacy. And however congenial a theme he found here, we feel the scene veiled, as it were, behind the artist's will to construction in terms of color.

In these two pictures what can be said to remain of classical Italian perspective and *trompe-l'œil?* Exactly nothing, apart from a semblance of depth—which however is purely imaginary. For what we have here is a new notion of space—that of modern painting—whose effect depends on a counterpoint of two-dimensional references. And figure and landscape are but different forms of the same signwork, the same brushwork.

Even at Saint-Rémy memories of Holland haunted Van Gogh (just as memories of Brittany haunted Gauguin in Tahiti), in a setting of reds, greens and virulent sunlight. On the other hand, he turned to a subdued, soothing yellow in rendering this *Peasant binding Wheat into Sheaves*, a theme he borrowed from Millet, imposing on it his own vision of color.

SELECT BIBLIOGRAPHY

Correspondence

Lettres à Emile Bernard, published by A. VOLLARD, Paris 1911; English translation, New York and London 1938. — *The Letters of a Post-Impressionist, being the Familiar Correspondence of V. v. G.*, with an introductory essay by A. M. LUDOVICI, London 1912. — *The Letters of V. v. G. to his Brother*, 1872-1886, with a Memoir by his sister-in-law, J. VAN GOGH-BONGER, New York and London 1927. — *Further Letters to his Brother*, 1886-1889, New York and London 1929. — *Lettres à son frère Théo*, selected by GEORGES PHILIPPART, introduction by CHARLES TERRASSE, Paris 1937. — *Brieven aan Ridder Van Rappard*, Amsterdam 1937. — *Letters to an Artist* (to Van Rappard), translated from the Dutch by RELA VAN MESSEL, introduction by WALTER PACH, New York 1936. — *Lettres à Van Rappard*, selected and translated by L. ROELANDT, Paris 1950. — *Briefe an Emile Bernard, Paul Gauguin, Paul Signac, und andere*, Basel 1938. — *Brieven aan zijn Broeder* (letters from Theo to Vincent), introduction by V. W. VAN GOGH, bibliography by J. VAN GOGH-BONGER, Amsterdam 1932.

Vincent VAN GOGH, *The Complete Letters,* 3 vols., edited by V. W. *N B* VAN GOGH, New York and London 1958.

Monographs

W. STEENHOFF, *V. G.*, Amsterdam 1905. — J. MEIER-GRAEFE, *Vincent*, Munich 1910. — H. P. BREMMER, *V. v. G., Inleidende Beschouwingen*, Amsterdam 1911. — E. H. DU QUESNE-VAN GOGH, *Personal Recollections of V. v. G.*, New York and London 1913. — W. HAUSENSTEIN, *V. G. und Gauguin*, Berlin 1914. — J. HAVELAAR, *V. v. G.*, Amsterdam 1915. — T. DURET, *V. G.*, Paris 1916. — C. GLASER, *V. v. G.*, Leipzig 1921. — J. KURODA, *Wan Gogu*, Tokyo 1921. — H. TIETZE, *V. v. G.*, Vienna 1922. — *V. v. G., a Biographical Study*, Medici Society, London 1922. — G. F. HARTLAUB, *V. v. G.*, Leipzig 1922. — K. PFISTER, *V. v. G.*, Potsdam 1922. — G. COQUIOT, *V. v. G.*, Paris 1923. — F. FELS, *V. G.*, Paris 1924. — R. GREY, *V. G.*, Rome and Paris 1924. — C. STERNHEIM, *Gauguin und V. G.*, Berlin 1924. — L. PIÉRARD, *La vie tragique de V. v. G.*, Paris 1924; second, revised edition, Paris 1939. — P. COLIN, *V. G.*, Paris 1925; English translation, New York 1926. — BENNO J. STOCKVIS, *Nasporingen omtrent V. v. G. in Brabant*, Amsterdam 1926. — J. B. DE LA FAILLE, *L'époque française de V. G.*, Paris 1927. — F. FELS, *V. v. G.*, Paris 1928. — J. MEIER-GRAEFE, *V. v. G. der Zeichner*, Berlin 1928. — S. STREICHER, *V. v. G.*, Zurich and Leipzig 1928. — V. CLEERDIN, *V. v. G. en Brabant*, Te 's Hertogenbosch 1929. — A. BERTRAM, *V. v. G.*,

London and New York 1929. — CH. TERRASSE, *V. G.*, Paris 1931. —
R. SHIKIBA *(V. v. G., his Life and Psychosis)*, Tokyo 1932. — G. KNUTTEL,
V. G. der Holländer, Stockholm 1932. — M. TINTI, *V. G.*, Bergamo 1933.
— J. MEIER-GRAEFE, *V. v. G., a Biographical Study*, New York 1933. —
P. J. S. BURRA, *V. G.*, London 1934. — T. W. EARP, *V. G.*, London and
Edinburgh. — CH. TERRASSE, *V. G. peintre*, Paris 1935. — H. WILM,
V. v. G., Munich 1935. — A. H. BARR, *V. v. G.*, New York 1935. —
✓ W. PACH, *V. v. G., a Study of the Artist and his Work in Relation to his Times*,
New York 1936. — L. VITALI, *V. v. G.*, Milan 1936. — W. UHDE, *V. v. G.*,
Vienna and Paris 1936. — G. L. LUZZATO, *V. v. G.*, Modena 1936. —
R. HUYGHE, *Les dessins de V. G.*, Paris 1937. — M. FLORISOONE, *V. G.*,
Paris 1937. — J. DE BEUCKEN, *V. v. G., un portrait*, Liège 1938. — B. GOLF,
V. G. og hans kunst, Copenhagen 1938. — A. M. ROSSET, *V. G.*, Paris
1941. — G. GRAPPE, *V. G.*, Paris 1941. — W. NIGG, *V. v. G.*, Bern
1942. — C. NORDENFALK, *V. v. G.*, Stockholm 1943. — R. JOSEPHSON,
V. v. G. naturalisten, Stockholm 1944. — L. HAUTECŒUR, *V. G.*, Monaco
1946. — J. SABILE, *V. G.*, Paris 1946. — P. JAMES, *V. G.*, London n. d.
(1946?). — J. C. VAN GELDER, *The Potato Eaters*, London n. d. — A. E.
JEWELL, *V. v. G.*, New York 1946. — F. ELGAR, *V. G., Peintures*, Paris
1947. — A. ARTAUD, *V. G., le suicidé de la société*, Paris 1947. — P. FIERENS,
V. G., Paris 1947. — P. COURTHION, *V. G. raconté par lui-même et par ses
amis, ses contemporains, sa postérité*, Geneva 1947. — F. HOLMER, *V. v. G.*,
Stockholm 1947. — A. RÜDLINGER, *V. v. G.*, Bern 1947. — A. PARRONCHI,
V. G., Florence 1947. — E. BRINER, *V. v. G.*, Zurich 1947. — Dr M. E.
TRALBAUT, *V. v. G. in zijn Antwerpsche Period*, Amsterdam 1948. —
W. MUENSTERBERGER, *V. v. G.*, Paris 1948. — A. M. HAMMACHER,
V. v. G., Amsterdam n. d. (1948?). — G. DUTHUIT, *V. G.*, Lausanne
1948. — G. SCHMIDT, *V. G.*, Bern 1948. — F. ELGAR, *V. G., Le Pont
de l'Anglois*, Paris 1948. — M. BUCHMANN, *Die Farbe bei V. v. G.*, Zurich
1948. — A. M. HAMMACHER, *V. v. G.*, Deventer n. d. (1948?). — A.
LECLERC, *V. G.*, Paris, London, New York n. d. (1949?). — F. ELGAR,
V. v. G., Paris 1949. — M. SHAPIRO, *V. v. G.*, New York 1950. —
J. DE LAPRADE, *V. G.*, Paris 1951. — J. COMBE, *V. v. G.*, Paris 1951. —
W. WEISBACH, *V. v. G., Kunst und Schicksal*, Basel 1949.

Catalogues

L'œuvre de Van Gogh, catalogue raisonné by J. B. DE LA FAILLE,
Paris and Brussels 1928; republished with a preface by CHARLES TERRASSE
(the paintings), Paris 1939. — *Van Gogh's Great Period: Arles, St. Rémy,
Auvers-sur-Oise*, by W. SCHERJON and J. DE GRUYTER, Amsterdam 1937. —
De Hollandsche Periode in het werk van Vincent van Gogh, by W. VANBE-
SELAERE, Amsterdam 1938. — *Catalogus van 264 Werken van Vincent van
Gogh, Rijksmuseum Kröller-Müller*, by A. M. HAMMACHER, Otterlo 1949.

EXHIBITIONS

In his lifetime: At the picture-dealers' Tanguy, rue Clauzel; Portier, rue Lepic; Thomas, boulevard Malesherbes; Martin, rue Mogador, Paris. — Salon des Indépendants, Paris 1888, 1889, 1890. — "Les Vingt", Brussels 1890.

After his death: Salon des Indépendants, Paris 1891. — "Les Vingt", Brussels 1891. — Gal. Le Barc de Boutteville, organized by Emile Bernard, Paris 1892. — Salle du Panorama, organized by J. Van Gogh-Bonger, preface by Roland Holst, Amsterdam 1892. — Copenhagen 1893. — The Hague, preface by Plasschaert, 1892. — Gal. Bernheim-Jeune, preface by Julien Leclercq, Paris 1901. — Salon des Indépendants, Paris 1905. — Stedelijk Museum, preface by Cohen-Gosschalk, Amsterdam 1905. — Gal. Arnold, Dresden 1905. — Hidde Nisland Collection, Dordrecht 1905. — Gal. Bernheim-Jeune, Paris 1908. — Gal. Druet, Paris 1908. — Gal. Brack, Munich 1909. — *Manet and the Post-Impressionists*, Grafton Galleries, preface by MacCarthy, London 1910. — Sonderbund, Cologne 1912. — Salon d'Automne, Paris 1912. — Gal. Cassirer, Berlin 1914. — Kunsthalle, Basel 1924. — Kunsthaus, preface by Wartmann, Zurich 1924. — Gal. Bernheim-Jeune, *L'époque française de V. G.*, preface by La Faille, Paris 1927. — Kröller-Müller Collection, The Hague 1927; same exhibition at Bern and Brussels 1927. — National Galerie, Berlin 1928. — Stedelijk Museum, *V. G. and his Contemporaries*, catalogue by La Faille, preface by Baard, Amsterdam 1930. — Traveling Exhibition, catalogue by A. H. Barr, U.S.A. 1935-1936. — Palais de Tokio, catalogue by M. Florisoone and J. Rewald, study by R. Huyghe, Paris 1937. — Stedelijk Museum, catalogue by W. Muensterberger, preface by H. L. Jaffé, Amsterdam 1945. — Traveling Exhibition, catalogue and preface by E. Langui, introduction by V. W. Van Gogh, Liège, Brussels, Mons 1946. — Musée de l'Orangerie, preface by R. Huyghe, Paris 1947; same exhibition, Musée Rath, Geneva 1947. — Kunsthalle, preface by L. Lichtenhahn, Basel 1947. — Boymans Museum, exhibition of drawings, Rotterdam 1947. — Traveling Exhibition, catalogue by Douglas Cooper, preface by Philip James, Tate Gallery, London, Art Gallery, Birmingham, Art Gallery, Glasgow 1948. — Municipal Museum, preface by D. de Gruyter, The Hague 1948. — Museum of Art, Cleveland 1948. — Traveling Exhibition, catalogue by T. Rousseau, preface by D. Catton Rich, Metropolitan Museum, New York, Art Institute, Chicago 1949-1950.— Traveling Exhibition, catalogue by M. Jauneau, studies by V. W. Van Gogh, M. Jullian, J. Leymarie, E. Leroy, Musée de Lyon, Musée de Grenoble, Arles, St.-Rémy 1951. — Stedelijk Museum, Amsterdam 1953. *we saw it in 1965*

LIST OF COLOR PLATES

INDEX OF NAMES